SPEECHCRAFT
An introduction to public speaking

BRENT C. OBERG

MERIWETHER PUBLISHING LTD.
Colorado Springs, Colorado

Meriwether Publishing Ltd., Publisher
P.O. Box 7710
Colorado Springs, CO 80933

Editor: Theodore O. Zapel
Typesetting: Susan Trinko
Cover design: Tom Myers

Library of Congress Cataloging-in-Publication Data

Oberg, Brent C. (Brent Christopher)
     Speechcraft : an introduction to public speaking / Brent C. Oberg.
  -- 1st ed.
        p.   cm.
  Includes bibliographical references.
     ISBN 1-56608-006-1 : $12.95
     1. Public Speaking.   I. Title.
PN4121.024   1994
808.5'1--dc20   94-21529
                                            CIP

To Beth

CONTENTS

Preface
Page vii

Preface

"How will this help me in the future?" This is a commonly asked question by students beginning a course in any discipline, and a reasonable one. After all, a course with no real-world application is certainly hard to justify. However, any course in beginning public speaking is essential and the skills learned in such a course will invariably be used by students in the future. It is impossible to even get a job unless one can make a good impression in an interview. Once employed, there are very few jobs and professions which do not require employees to speak or present themselves in one way or another. As a top advertising executive says, "Business is presentation." Therefore, as you progress through the beginning speech class, you may find it difficult and even nerve-racking, but will also find it to be beneficial and rewarding.

This text provides practical instruction, relevant activities, and formal assignments designed to help you learn the skills of effective presentation. The handbook is divided into chapters, each of which supports one or two clear, specific, instructional objectives. Each chapter begins with an introduction, which explains the objectives and purposes of the material in that chapter. Following each introduction are notes on the theory, research, and beliefs of the topics of that chapter. Following the instruction notes are ideas for individual and group classroom activities supporting the objectives of the chapter. These are activities that most likely cannot be used as formal speech assignments, but allow for practice on the skills that will be used on the formal assignments in that chapter. Next come the formal speech assignments which require you to display the knowledge and skills you have learned in the chapter.

The material in this textbook is based on extensive research as well as my own experience as a speaker and a teacher of speech. I hope you will find this text clear, easy to use, and helpful in developing essential speech skills. Most importantly, this is a resource *for you*. Therefore, you should use it in the manner it will benefit you the most. Good luck!

Communication Apprehension

Overcoming ApprehensionThrough
Introductory Public Speaking Activities

Introduction

In 1973, R. H. Bruskin Associates, a marketing research firm, conducted a national survey in which respon-
dents were asked to rank a list of items that would cause
them anxiety or fear. The number one fear among American
adults was found to be speaking in public, ranking ahead
of deep water, financial problems, height, insects, and even
death. To anyone who has ever had to deliver a speech before
an audience, this may not be surprising. Stage fright, more
formally known as communication apprehension, is very
common. Hardly anyone is able to perform in front of an
audience without some degree of fear and nervousness. Says
Ron Hoff, "If you're alive, your nervous system is going to
be going full throttle, or close to it, when you get up to
present yourself." This is also true for students in public
speaking courses. Many teachers of beginning speech believe
that communication apprehension, more than any other factor, causes public speaking students to perform poorly.

Communication apprehension is defined by Mary Hinchcliff Pelias of Southern Illinois University as "an individual's level of fear or anxiety associated with either real or
anticipated communication with another person or persons."
However, such nervousness need not get in the way of effective presentation. Therefore, the purpose of this chapter is
to provide practical suggestions and activities that will allow
you to understand and control the apprehension you feel
when called upon to present. The material in this chapter
is based on a belief that three separate factors can help
speakers overcome communication apprehension. These are
knowledge of how to deal with nervousness, being distracted
while speaking, and success in initial public speaking situations.

The instructional notes discuss the nature of stage
fright, give practical suggestions for dealing with nervous-

ness, and give suggestions for the use of visual aids in a presentation. The activities and assignments are designed to give you a high chance for success as they primarily deal with introductions. This allows you to deliver initial presentations on yourself, a subject you know better than anyone else. Also, as you become better acquainted with your classmates, you will feel less anxiety speaking before them. The exceptions to this are the demonstration speech and the visual aid speech. You may wonder why these assignments are included in this section of this book. The answer to this is simple: these speeches require the use of visual aids. For many speakers, this tends to reduce nervousness as they become more focused on their visuals and what they are showing the audience and less focused on their fear. In short, visuals can distract from nervousness.

For almost all students entering a beginning speech course, nervousness and fear are primary concerns. This chapter provides suggestions for dealing with fear and activities that demonstrate it is possible to present despite stage fright. By the end of this chapter, you will have dealt effectively with your first major hurdle in public speaking: communication apprehension.

COMMUNICATION APPREHENSION

If you feel nervous, apprehensive, and worried before you speak in public, you are not alone. In fact, you're in good company: notable actors and performers such as Johnny Carson, Sir Lawrence Olivier, Helen Hayes, Maureen Stapleton, Luciano Pavarotti, and Willard Scott have also suffered from stage fright, or communication apprehension, as it is also called. Hollywood actor George C. Scott, famous for his roles as General Patton and Dicken's Scrooge, describes what he goes through when he is called upon to give a speech. Says Scott, "It's terrible when I have to make a speech. I really suffer. I'm a nervous wreck. When I get up, I shake all over like a dog shaking the water off." In fact, surveys show that speaking before a group is the number one fear of American adults. However, if you understand the cause of your fear and know practical suggestions for controlling your nervousness while speaking, you can overcome your stage fright and perhaps even use it to your advantage.

Reasons for Nervousness

Understanding the reasons for your nervousness is the first step to controlling it.

1. ***Fear of being stared at.*** Many people are uncomfortable being the center of attention. When you are speaking, like it or not, that is exactly what you are.

2. ***Fear of failure.*** Many speakers allow questions such as "What if I make a fool of myself?" and "What if I mess up?" to affect their performance.

3. ***Fear of rejection.*** Have you ever called a member of the opposite sex and asked for a date? If you have, you know how fast your heart races, how your palms become sweaty, and how a lump forms in your throat. This is because no one likes to be rejected. When you ask for a date — or

5

speak before an audience — you are asking for acceptance and approval and will naturally be nervous.

4. *Fear of the unknown.* If you are not familiar with public speaking, it is a new experience. Typically, new experiences cause fear.

So is it hopeless, then? Do these factors make it impossible for you to speak in public? Absolutely not! Even though fear is normal, you can overcome it! In fact, in many cases, it may even help you.

The Value of Fear

1. *Fear gives you energy.* When you are nervous, your energy level picks up. This can make you more enthusiastic and interesting while speaking. If you play sports, you've probably felt this effect. Butterflies before a game can turn into energy during the game that allows you to play better than you normally would. Hamilton Gregory believes this is why teams that are heavily favored are often upset by lesser teams. The favorites are too relaxed while the underdogs become "pumped" with emotion.

2. *Nervousness shows respect for your audience.* After all, if you are nervous, that tells the audience that they are worth being nervous about. In this way, nervousness can help a speaker build a rapport with an audience.

How to Control Your Nervousness When Speaking

Knowing how to deal with your nervousness is the best tool you have to control it. What follows are ten techniques that can relax you before you speak. They may not all work for you: the trick is to find those that do and use them!

1. *Don't fight your fear.* Realize that it is completely natural for you to be nervous. Believe that it can help you.

2. *Walk before presenting.* If it is possible, go for a brisk

walk before you present. Even if it's just in the hall between classes, exercise can relax you. According to Ron Hoff, walking before presenting will loosen up your whole body and prevent you from shaking during presentations.

3. **Don't cross your legs while you are preparing to speak.** If you do, the leg on the bottom may fall asleep and won't support you when you get up to speak.

4. **Dangle your arms and twirl your wrists while waiting to speak.** Let your arms dangle loosely at your sides. Twirl your wrists gently to shake off nervous energy. You've seen athletes do this before games. It can loosen a speaker up the same way it can an athlete.

5. **Take deep breaths before you speak.** This also relaxes you and gives you the air you so desperately need when you are nervous.

6. **Choose a topic you like.** If you are excited about what you are going to say, you will be less likely to worry about how you will say it. You may even be *excited* to share your topic with the audience. (I know this may not seem likely now, but it does happen!)

7. **Be prepared.** The more you know about a topic, the less likely you are to forget anything. The less likely you are to forget your speech, the less nervous you will be. Likewise, the more you have practiced, the more confidence you will feel.

8. **Imagine yourself speaking well.** Another technique athletes use that can also help speakers is positive visualization. Before you speak, close your eyes and imagine yourself giving a strong, fluent speech. Pretend you are Martin Luther King and Abraham Lincoln rolled into one. If you picture yourself being successful, you're more likely to actually be successful.

9. **Don't call attention to your nervousness.** As the commercial says, "Never let them see you sweat." If you are

openly uncomfortable, the audience will be less likely to listen to you and to respect you. You might even make *them* nervous! Also, if you act confident, you may trick yourself into being confident!

10. ***Don't be afraid to make mistakes.*** Many speakers worry that even one mistake will ruin their entire speech. Think about this: how many times in normal conversation do you stop and correct yourself? Does it ruin a conversation? Of course, everyone makes many mistakes in conversation, and most go completely unnoticed. The same is true of speeches. If you make a mistake, correct yourself and go on. It's far more important and realistic for you to deal with mistakes well than to avoid them completely.

USING VISUAL AIDS EFFECTIVELY

If used properly, visual aids can add much to a presentation. They make your speech more interesting, provide additional information and support, and help your audience remember the presentation. However, if used incorrectly, they can distract from the performance and damage the credibility of the speaker.

Using Visual Aids in a Speech

1. ***Have your visuals prepared ahead of time.*** As a speaker, you should always treat your audience with respect. To take their time to set up your visuals is very rude. A student who did a demonstration speech on how to make an Orange Julius was progressing fine until about midway through his presentation. He then looked up and exclaimed, "Oh, no!" Then, without a word of explanation, he ran out the door. After about ten seconds, he returned with a cup full of water. He continued, "You then add a cup of water . . ." While this is an extreme (but true) example, it shows what can happen when visuals are not prepared ahead of time.

2. **Make sure the entire audience can see your visuals.** Not only should your visuals be large enough for your entire audience to see, but they must be placed in a spot that affords the entire audience visibility. Again, to expect your audience to move or "gather 'round" shows a lack of consideration.

3. **Be sure visuals can be manipulated quickly in a speech.** There should not be long pauses while you set up your visuals or manipulate them in a speech. For instance, many students have done cooking demonstrations that require thirty to sixty seconds of stirring time. Thus, the audience spends up to a full minute watching the speaker stir. Again, this can be avoided through preparation. For instance, a speaker could have a separate mixture pre-stirred.

   If a lengthy manipulation is absolutely necessary, plan material to discuss while you demonstrate. One student, while demonstrating how to make a homemade pizza, told the history of pizza and explained the differences between types of pizza while he was rolling his dough.

4. **Visuals should be neat and professional looking.** Just as your dress communicates much about your attitude, so do your visuals. Charts that are sloppily drawn show that you have spent little time and energy in the preparation of your speech. Neat visuals show your effort and tell the audience that you care enough about them to take time preparing your speech.

5. **Practice using visuals a number of times before using them in a speech.** Visuals can act in strange and mysterious ways if you aren't comfortable manipulating them. Posters can fall over, objects can be dropped, tapes can be at the wrong point. Be sure to practice with your visuals to avoid these distracting mistakes.

CLASSROOM ACTIVITIES

Individual and Group Activities to Help Speakers Overcome Communication Apprehension and Become Acquainted With One Another

OBJECTIVES

Speakers will gain experience speaking in front of large groups and begin to reduce the apprehension they feel when called upon to speak.

Introduction of a Friend

The instructor divides the class into groups of two. You will interview your partner, asking questions similar to the following:

1. What is your name?

2. What grade are you in?

3. How long have you lived in your current home? If you have lived anywhere else, where?

4. What is your favorite sport?

5. What is your favorite flavor of ice cream?

6. What is your biggest pet peeve?

Take four to five minutes to interview your partner. When finished, go to the front of the room, introduce your partner, and allow your partner to introduce you.

Personal Collage

Prepare a collage on a piece of posterboard that displays your name, a picture of you, and pictures (either original drawings, photographs, or pictures cut from magazines) that reflect your interests, hobbies, and lifestyle. You will then explain your collage to the class in a brief presentation. Collages can be kept and displayed in the classroom to enable students as well as the instructor to remember the names and characteristics of the individuals in the class.

Personal Interview

Find a partner with whom you can work. Alone, prepare a list of ten to fifteen "probing questions" to ask your partner. One by one, the groups will take seats at the front of the class and conduct the interviews. Take turns acting as the interviewer, completing one entire interview before changing roles. The list of prepared questions can serve as a guide, but if a response to one question brings up a particularly interesting issue, you can leave your list of prepared questions to ask a "follow-up question." It is important, to make this activity fun and interesting, that you try to ask creative and original questions when serving as the interviewer.

Object Speech

Bring one object that is either special to you for some reason or that reflects your personality and interests. In a short speech, explain the nature and history of the object, and relate its importance to your personality. This activity not only provides a speaking experience, but can also be good practice for anyone who eventually will have to deliver either a demonstration or a visual aid speech.

ASSIGNMENTS

An Explanation of the Objectives and Purposes of the Assignments Designed to Support the Material Dealing With Overcoming Communication Apprehension

Introductory Speech

The introductory speech is designed as the initial assignment in a public speaking course. Because it is the first speech given in a class, and in many cases one of the first speeches ever given, there will be a great deal of anxiety surrounding this assignment. However, it should be made easier by the subject matter as it deals with the subject everyone knows the most about: him or herself. It is a beneficial assignment as it provides an initial speech assignment with a subject that is easy to speak on and allows the members of a class to become more comfortable and familiar with each other.

OBJECTIVES

1. To promote self-confidence in speech by providing an initial public speaking experience with a high probability of success.

2. To build comfort for participants in a public speaking classroom by allowing you to become acquainted with your fellow students.

3. To provide the instructor with a diagnostic measurement of the students' initial competence in public speaking at the onset of a course.

Demonstration and Visual Aid Speeches

These speeches are very similar as they both require the use and manipulation of visual aids and outside materials. As previously mentioned, these assignments are placed in the opening section of this handbook as they can greatly help control communication apprehension. As speakers focus more on the demonstration and the manipulation of their visual aids, they focus less on their fear of speaking in public. Also, these speeches are often more enjoyable for the audience as they deal with interesting subject matter and give the audience something to watch.

OBJECTIVES

1. To help beginning speakers overcome communication apprehension and stage fright by allowing them to focus on the manipulation of visuals rather than their fear.

2. To demonstrate how visual aids clarify the content of a speech and make a speech more interesting.

3. To help you learn the proper techniques of preparing visuals for use in a public speaking situation and the proper means of manipulating visuals within a speech.

ASSIGNMENT
Introductory Speech

Assignment

Deliver a speech introducing yourself to the class in a creative way. By the end of the speech, we should be acquainted with you, but you must find a way of introducing yourself that is more creative than simply, "Hi, my name is . . ., my hobbies are . . ." (You get the picture.)

Ideas for Making Your Speech Creative

1. Tell a story that shows your character or personality.
   (If you are generous, tell of a time you helped someone; if you are lazy, tell about a time you got out of work, etc.)

2. Pretend you are someone else describing you.
   (You could speak from the perspective of your best friend, your parent, your pet, or anyone else who knows you and therefore let us know what others might think of you.)

3. Deliver a eulogy.
   (Act as if you are speaking at your own funeral. You could describe your untimely demise, tell what you accomplished during your short time on earth, and what you had hoped for from the future you cannot now live.)

4. Come up with your own idea.
   (Remember — have fun and be creative.)

Topics to Discuss and Questions to Answer in Your Speech

1. State your name.

2. Tell about your childhood. Where have you lived? When did you move to your current home? Were there any events that had a special effect upon you?

3. Tell about your plans for the future. What do you hope for out of life?

14

4. Describe your hobbies and interests. How do you spend your spare time?

5. What activities are you involved in at school?

6. Tell anything else that is important for us to know about you.

Other Requirements

TIME: 2 to 3 minutes

DUE DATE:

Demonstration Speech

Assignment

Deliver a speech that informs, or teaches, your audience how to do something. In addition to *telling* your audience how something is done, you will use visuals to *show* them through demonstration. You will be graded on your organization, presentation skills, thoroughness of preparation, and how well you manipulate visuals. After seeing your demonstration, we should be able to duplicate the process you have shown us.

Topic Ideas

You may speak on any topic you choose. The best topics are those that are original and deal with things that most people don't already know how to do. For instance, how to make a peanut butter sandwich is not a good topic as almost everyone already knows how to do it and will therefore be bored watching a speech on it. A list of ideas follows. Remember, these are only ideas — you are not required to choose from this list.

1. How to cook an original dish (a dessert, a quick snack, etc.)
2. How to wrap a present
3. How to make original Christmas presents
4. How to make a craft item (cross-stitch, candles, etc.)
5. How to administer CPR
6. How to diaper a baby
7. How to braid hair
8. How to make a woodworking project
9. How to perform magic

10. How synthesizers are used

11. How to make objects in origami

Other Requirements

You must speak from an outline, not a script. You will be required to turn in your outline at the conclusion of your speech.

TIME: 3 to 5 minutes

DUE DATE:

ASSIGNMENT
Visual Aid Speech

Assignment

Deliver a speech that either teaches your audience about a subject or how to do something, persuades or motivates them, or entertains them. To enhance your presentation, you will use at least one visual aid. The primary consideration in the selection and construction of a visual aid is that it contributes to the content of your speech and clarifies the information you are giving the audience.

A visual aid may be a chart, graph, picture, object, video slide show, etc. However, you must prepare your visual ahead of time. Therefore, you cannot use the chalkboard.

Topic Ideas

You may speak on any topic you choose. Below is a list of ideas — remember these are only ideas; you are not restricted to this list.

1. Demonstrate how something is done (cooking, making a craft, repairing a bicycle, etc.)

2. Persuade us to a certain point of view on a current issue. Use a graph or chart to show supporting facts or statistics.

3. Teach us the history of a certain event, time period, etc. Use pictures to make your information more concrete.

Other Requirements

You must speak from an outline, not a script. You will be required to turn your outline in at the conclusion of your speech.

TIME: 3 to 5 minutes

DUE DATE:

Techniques of Delivery

The Principles of
Effective Presentation Techniques

Introduction

Traditionally, the art of public speaking has been broken down into two components: content and delivery. Simply put, content is what you say while delivery is how you say it. The purpose of this chapter is to help you develop your skills in the latter of these two categories: the delivery and presentation of speeches. It has been suggested that "presentation is everything." While this may be something of an exaggeration, it is certainly true that the manner in which a speech is received has a tremendous amount to do with the way it is presented. Think of the individuals throughout history who are known for their oratorical skills: Martin Luther King, Jr., Patrick Henry, Abraham Lincoln. While the words of these great men have certainly lived on, they will always be remembered for their composure, strength, and conviction as they have presented speeches.

However, speech students at the high school and college level have seen and perhaps even given thousands of presentations. Common sense and experience have taught them that an effective speaker uses a clear, well-inflected voice, stands up straight, makes eye contact with the audience, and so on. For this reason, the activities in this chapter are just as vital as the instruction as they provide you an opportunity to refine skills you already know. Further, the two can be used together, as the activities can illustrate a point made in instruction and help you to practice aspects of speaking on which you may need additional improvement.

You will notice there are no formal assignments provided in this chapter. This is because the concepts taught in this chapter are so fundamental to public speaking that they will inevitably be dealt with continually throughout an entire speech course. They are not something to be learned and forgotten, or to be used only in certain speech situations. The principles of effective delivery are essential for all speakers in all speech situations.

21

TECHNIQUES OF DELIVERY

Delivery, or the manner in which you present a speech, can be vitally important. How many times have you mentally "turned off" speakers because you did not like their appearance, manner, or did not think they showed sufficient composure? Have you ever found yourself excited or persuaded by speakers because they demonstrated such strength and conviction you couldn't help but be moved? Naturally, both these situations arise continually and demonstrate the impact a speaker's delivery can have upon his or her presentation. Here we will cover the major components of a speaker's presentation style that can add much to the strength of delivery.

Charisma

Charisma, or "presence," is a hard quality to define and an even harder one to identify. However, when a speaker has it, you know. Charisma refers to the manner in which speakers carry themselves; how they are perceived by their audiences. When you are presenting, the audience will watch you and make judgments about you even before you open your mouth to speak. Cristina Stuart, author of *How to Be an Effective Speaker*, makes this point by saying, "Consider your own internal conversations as you sit in a railway station or an airport lounge — aren't you assessing and criticizing everyone you see?" Quite simply, an audience is curious about anyone to whom they will spend some time listening and will inevitably make judgments about such a person.

So, as a presenter, you will be on display. You will be the center of attention. You naturally want to make a good impression and be perceived by the audience as a presenter with charisma, or presence. But how do you do this? Ron Hoff, author of *I Can See You Naked*, makes a number of suggestions to help presenters "get some presence."

1. ***Presenters with "presence" have a sense of purpose.*** Nothing is tentative. They walk briskly. They know where they are going and why they are going there.

2. ***They are open to the audience.*** Presenters with presence have an open, outward attitude. They are aware of their surroundings and interested in the people around them. They move *into* an audience, rather than seeming detached from it.

3. ***They project a positive attitude.*** They seem to want to present. They are excited about what they have to say and the people to whom they will say it.

4. ***They look good.*** Their dress and appearance shows that they care enough about the audience to get dressed up a little, to make themselves look nice.

Gestures: Using Your Hands

Normally, our arms and hands are a useful, functional part of our bodies. We don't typically give much thought to how they should be used or where they should be placed. However, there are instances when our hands and arms can get in the way and seem awkward. Have you ever noticed that sometimes when you go to bed, there seems to be no right place to put your arms? No matter what you do, they seem to be in the way. This phenomenon can also occur when you present. Often, there seems to be no appropriate place to put your hands or nothing that should be done with them. To help, here is a list of dos and don'ts:

1. ***Don't fidget with your hands.*** Fiddling with rings, cuffs, buttons, pens, your notes, the lectern, your hair, or anything else within reach shows your nervousness and distracts from your presentation.

2. ***Don't touch your face, hair, or clothes.***

3. ***Don't hide your hands*** by putting them in pockets, behind your back, or by folding your arms.

4. *__Don't__ wring or rub your hands together nervously.*

5. *__Do__ use gestures.* Gestures add emphasis to important points in your speech, give your presentation visual interest, and, as Hoff points out, "prove you're alive."

6. *__Don't__ use too many gestures.* If you gesture too often, the gestures lose their impact and can be distracting. If you have a tendency to do this, a suggestion made by Hoff might help. Stand in front of a full-length mirror with a heavy book (such as a dictionary) in each hand. At times, you will still raise your hands in a gesture despite the heavy books. These are the gestures that are essential and should be left in your speech. However, because of the weight of the books, you will be discouraged from using any extraneous gestures or movements.

7. *__Don't__ repeat a gesture too often.* Speakers will sometimes use the same gesture over and over. Try for a wide variety of gestures.

8. *__Do__ keep your hands at your sides when not using gestures.* When you are not gesturing, the most effective thing to do with your hands is to let them fall comfortably at your sides. Though this may feel awkward and stiff, it looks very professional. If you are using a lectern, you may rest your hands gently on the lectern, but be careful not to lean or to expect the lectern to support your weight.

9. *__Do__ make your gestures above your waist.* Gestures made below the waist tend to look less professional and more lazy than those at waist level or higher.

Facial Expressions

Your face can be extremely expressive and appropriate facial expressions can add much to a presentation. Be careful, however, not to overdo it. Usually, if you feel strongly about your topic and if you are making effective eye contact as opposed to reading from a script, facial expressions will come naturally.

Eye Contact

Eye contact is crucial for a speaker. Ron Hoff asserts, "Vocal cords may carry your message, but eyes hold your audience." By making effective eye contact with an audience, you establish a relationship with them and show you are interested in their responses and feedback. If you doubt how important eye contact is in relationship building, consider this: have you ever seen two people, perhaps a husband and wife or boyfriend and girlfriend, involved in an argument? It is not uncommon for people who are arguing to turn from each other and avoid eye contact. However, if you have ever watched a couple having a romantic dinner, you will see quite the opposite. They will lean across the table toward each other, gazing deeply into each other's eyes. These examples prove that we tend to engage in eye contact with those we care about and those with whom we are comfortable. Therefore, if a speaker avoids eye contact with his or her audience, what message does that send? So how can you increase eye contact? Here are some ideas:

1. ***Do not write out speeches word for word.*** If you use a complete script, you will need to read and will not be able to look at your audience as often.

2. ***There is no set period of time to make eye contact with each member of the audience.*** Though some people will assert that you should look at each member of the audience for three or five seconds then move on, this is a fallacy. If you try to do this, you will concentrate on counting rather than your message or the feedback of your audience. It is far more important that you attempt to make a "connection" with the members of your audience.

3. ***Include all members of the audience.*** When presenting, there is a natural tendency to give more attention to audience members in the front and center sections of the audience. However, you need to remember that *all* members of your audience are important and shouldn't be

ignored. Once, in an interview, Garth Brooks was asked why audiences respond so well to his performances. Brooks said that he goes to an arena before a show, stands on the stage, and looks at the last seat in the last row of the highest balcony. He then tries to decide what he will do in the show to make that person feel special, to make them feel as if they are in the front row. We can all learn from Garth Brooks. No, we don't have to all become balding country singers, but we can make a point of using eye contact to make everyone in the audience feel involved in our presentation.

Voice

Clearly, *speakers* have to be able to use their *voices* effectively! Joseph A. DeVito, author of *The Elements of Public Speaking*, breaks down the vocal elements of delivery into the following components:

1. **Volume.** You should speak at an appropriate volume for the room in which you are presenting. If you are in a fairly large room, you need to project your voice so you can be heard clearly by the person farthest from you. An experiment can illustrate how you need to project differently for different situations. Pretend you are trying to gain the attention of someone seated in the next chair by calling a name. Now, pretend that person is across the room. Call them again, increasing your volume accordingly. Finally, pretend the person you are calling to is outside the room you are in and call to them once more. You can see how you need to vary volume depending on how far your audience is from you. It is important to note that your volume does vary. Many speakers use a loud volume, no matter how small the room in which they are presenting. If you are in a small room, speak no louder than you would in normal conversation with your audience members — don't overpower them.

2. **Rate.** Rate refers to the speed with which you speak. Be

careful that your rate is neither too slow nor too fast. If it is too slow, your listeners' minds may wander from your presentation; if it is too fast, your audience may not be able to follow or understand you. More often, presenters will speak too quickly as that can be a result of nervousness. If you struggle with this, planning pauses where you can remind yourself to slow down periodically through your presentation can help.

3. *Vocal Variety and Inflection.* This refers to the amount of variance in pitch, which is defined as the relative highness or lowness of your voice. Though you don't want to overdo it, it is preferable to have a good amount of vocal variance, rather than a monotone pitch. It adds interest to your presentation and helps emphasize important points.

4. *Articulation and Pronunciation.* Articulation is the way we physically form a word, while pronunciation refers to how closely we state a word in accordance with some accepted standard, such as a dictionary. It is vital that speakers both articulate words clearly and pronounce them correctly. If you need to say a word in a speech and do not know the correct pronunciation, look it up. It is much better to take the time to do this than to mispronounce a word during a presentation.

5. *Pauses.* Pauses are important as they help emphasize important points, give the audience time to process information, and allow time for laughter if a joke is used. However, speakers tend to be uncomfortable with silence and will often use "filler words" such as "um," "er," "you know," and "like." We've all known people who do this to excess and have seen how distracting it can be. I've known students who will count the number of times an instructor uses a certain filler in a class period rather than taking notes. Further, we are so accustomed to using these fillers that we are usually not even aware of when

we do. Thus, being aware of when we use fillers and making a concerted effort to eliminate them can normally be quite effective.

Other Characteristics of Effective Delivery

There are several other characteristics of effective delivery not mentioned above. Following are several techniques that will help you speak more effectively:

1. *Try to be natural.* I once heard a speech teacher praising one of his students. He said, "She speaks as if she is addressing only one person, a friend, no matter how large her audience." Speakers should always appear relaxed and natural, not as if they are "giving a speech."

2. *Reinforce your message.* Your gestures, expressions, and use of vocal techniques should all contribute to the tone and content of your message.

3. *Vary your delivery.* Avoid repetitive and predictable patterns. Try to vary your vocal expression as well as the energy of your presentation.

4. *Use a conversational style.* In normal conversation, we are spontaneous, make eye contact, and are responsive to feedback. Effective presenters also embody these characteristics.

Rehearsal Techniques

It is absolutely, positively essential that you practice and rehearse a speech before you present it. Can you imagine how a football team would perform if they tried to play a game with no practice? What if an ensemble attempted to stage a play, but didn't bother to rehearse? Obviously, both situations would be complete disasters. However, many presenters attempt to speak without any or sufficient practice, even though they are every bit as much performers as athletes or actors. So, how do you practice correctly?

1. ***Engage in both mental and physical rehearsal.*** According-ing to Frank E. X. Dance and Carol C. Zak-Dance, co-authors of *Public Speaking*, both types of practice can provide great benefits. By mental rehearsal, they suggest visualizing yourself mentally presenting a strong, poised, coherent presentation. This is a technique that is often used by athletes with sometimes stunning results. The theory is that if you picture yourself speaking effectively, you will indeed speak effectively. Physical rehearsal is the more common type of practice where a speaker pre-sents his speech to a friend, coworker, or simply to the wall. It is this type of rehearsal with which the remainder of the suggestions for practice will be concerned.

2. ***Rehearse the speech as a whole.*** It is better to not prac-tice sections of a speech individually. After all, you don't present your speech in sections. It is often beneficial to go so far as to practice your speech just as it will be performed, from the moment you get out of your seat to speak until the time you have returned to your seat.

3. ***Simulate the speaking situation as closely as possible.*** The ideal situation is to practice your speech in the very room in which it will be performed. If this is not possible, try to find a room or environment as close to the perform-ance environment as possible. If a lectern will be used, use one in practice. Just do anything you can to make your practice approximate the actual performance.

4. ***Watch yourself perform.*** Often, we do not realize that we make a certain mistake until we see ourselves do it. For instance, one speech student demonstrated a nervous mannerism through all of his speeches. No matter how many times he was told of this tendency, he persisted in using it. Finally, he was videotaped and allowed to see himself perform. While watching the tape, he replied (rather candidly), "I look awful!" He never used the dis-tracting mannerism again. Videotaping is the best way

to watch yourself speak, but if a camera is not available, speaking into a full-length mirror or even audiotaping your speech can also be useful.

5. **Make notes on your speech.** Write suggestions to yourself on your script or delivery notes. If you have a tendency to speak too quickly, write "Slow down!" in the margin of your script. If you want to emphasize a certain word or phrase, underline it. If you intend to move at a certain point in your speech, indicate this on your notes. If you fail to do this, you'll be amazed at how easy it will be to forget these things while speaking.

6. **Time yourself.** Chances are, no matter the situation in which you will be speaking, there will be a time limit on your presentation. You cannot know how closely your speech comes to that limit until you time yourself in practice.

7. **Rehearse often.** The more you practice, the stronger your delivery becomes. Also, the more you rehearse a speech successfully, the more confidence you will have, making yourself less likely to become nervous.

8. **Rehearse anywhere.** Take any opportunity to practice your speech. Rehearse in the shower, while driving, etc. I used to practice my speeches on walks. Eventually, I had to discontinue this after the neighbors questioned my mental health. However, the important point is to practice as much as you can.

Learning how to properly deliver a speech is not an easy task. There are many techniques to learn and distractions such as nervousness can hinder your ability to speak well in public. However, anyone can master the techniques of effective delivery if they are aware of what to do, how to practice effectively, and willing to work to improve.

CLASSROOM ACTIVITIES

Individual and Group Activities to Help Speakers Refine the Skills of Presentation

OBJECTIVES

The following activities allow an opportunity to practice the skills of effective speech presentation and to remedy common errors in delivery through enjoyable games and activities.

The Stare Down

Even though eye contact is vitally important, it is something with which we sometimes feel uncomfortable, especially if we are nervous, as we may be while speaking. The stare down can help you overcome the anxiety you feel when asked to make eye contact with class members and other audience members.

Find a partner. Your task is to look into your partner's eyes for a full two minutes. Blinking is allowed, but talking, laughing, looking away, and touching aren't. A technique that is sometimes helpful is to conduct this activity twice, choosing your partner the first time and being randomly assigned to a partner the second. The reason for this is that when you choose a partner, you will probably choose someone you know well, which makes the assignment easier. However, when partners are assigned, you may be paired with someone you don't know well, which is a more uncomfortable situation. The class might decide to make this activity more interesting by making a contest out of the exercise, with the winners being the group that can stare at each other the longest or the groups that can make it to a certain time limit, such as two minutes.

The idea is that if you can make direct eye contact with one person without speaking for an extended period of time, you can look at a member of an audience during a speech

31

for a few seconds without feeling uneasy.

Making Eye Contact With the Entire Audience

As noted in the instruction in this chapter, speakers often have a tendency to spend more time looking at audience members in the front and center sections of the audience. This drill illustrates this and demonstrates the importance of looking at all members of an audience.

Each student will be called to the front of the class to speak and given a simple impromptu topic such as "my family," "football," or "horses." As you speak on your subject, you are required to make eye contact with every member of the audience. As you make direct eye contact with members of the audience, the audience members must raise their hands. You must continue speaking until everyone in the room has raised his or her hand.

This activity has the additional advantage of demonstrating the importance of being an active, involved listener.

The "Um" Game

Students usually find this game, which helps you to speak without filler words, very enjoyable. Each student is called to the front of the class and given an impromptu topic. You are required to speak on your topic for as long as possible without using "um," "uh," "er," "you know," or any other filler. The speaker that can speak the longest may be offered a prize or reward.

This activity demonstrates how often fillers are used by speakers and the necessity of cutting down on the number of fillers used in speech.

The Truth/Lie Game

Think of a story about yourself that is either true or a lie. Then write down either "Truth" or "Lie" on a piece of scratch paper and hand it to the instructor before telling your story to the class. After you tell your story, the class will vote to see how many people believe it to be true. Your job as a speaker is to fool as many of your classmates as possible. Thus, you must either tell a lie that sounds like something that could have actually happened or a true story that sounds outrageous. The top speaker will be the individual that fools the most people.

When the class votes to determine how many believe a story to be true, only one vote should be taken for each student. For instance, after an individual student presents, the instructor could ask how many people believe the story to be true and then determine how many believe it to be a lie by subtracting from the total number of students in the class. This prevents students from not voting and skewing the results. Also, no one should leave the room during this activity as it changes the number of students voting and also makes the results inconsistent.

Expert Speech Evaluations

One of the most effective ways for any aspiring speaker to learn how to effectively present a speech is to watch expert speakers and use them as models. By watching such examples, either in the form of videos or advanced speech students, or by attending functions at which an address is made, you can do much to learn the principles of effective speech-making.

Diaphragmatic Breathing

Carol Marrs, author of *The Complete Book of Speech Communication*, suggests an activity to help illustrate the importance of breathing from the diaphragm (the large muscle at the bottom of the rib cage that allows you to control your breathing). In this activity, you must select one page of writing from a novel, textbook, etc. You will then stand at the front of the class and read as much of the text as possible while using only a single breath. It is important to stress that your words should be easily heard and understood by all class members. This activity can also be made into a contest, with the winner being the student who can speak for the longest period of time in a single breath.

Videotaped Speeches

Videotaping speeches can have tremendous benefits as it allows you to analyze yourself as a speaker and see your strengths and areas of needed improvement. Any speech in a course may be taped, but shorter speeches are usually most effective as the entire class is often forced to watch both the taping and the playback of the speeches.

There are two ways in which you can learn from a video of yourself speaking. First, your instructor or another person who knows the principles of public speaking can take the video and evaluate it, and then use the video to illustrate and reinforce feedback to you. Another effective technique is to view your own video and make an honest self-evaluation (you may use the speech evaluation form in Chapter Three if you wish). Often, you are more likely to correct a mistake in your speaking style if you identify that mistake yourself.

Effective Delivery Skit

This activity not only requires thinking about the question, "What is effective delivery?", it also provides another opportunity for you to present in an enjoyable, non-threatening situation. In a group of three to five students, present a short skit that demonstrates or teaches, in some way, effective speech delivery. The skits should be as original and creative as possible and may include ideas such as rap songs, the creation of a fake speech classroom, a commercial for a "Speech School," or the performance of a television talk show.

Practice Diary

An interesting activity to help develop effective practice techniques is to keep a diary of your practice program for any particular speech. Note how many times and for how long you practiced, when you first felt you were ready to perform for an audience, if you practiced in front of anyone, and any techniques you found especially helpful. This activity makes you more aware of which practice techniques are most useful and successful for you.

Listening Skills

Learning the Skills of Critical Listening

Introduction

Adlai Stevenson once began a speech by saying, "My assignment is to talk to you for a while, and yours is to listen to me. I trust we will both finish our work at the same time." In this statement, Stevenson draws what seems to be an obvious conclusion. However, anyone who has ever taught a speech class can testify that listeners often finish their work long before a speaker concludes. This is a critical problem because listening is an essential skill for individuals to learn in order to become effective communicators. The purpose of this chapter is to provide you with opportunities to learn the skills of critical listening that are so important in so many aspects of communication.

There are three major benefits of learning critical listening skills. First, it develops critical thinking, argumentation, and speaking skills. Simply, it is impossible to respond to an argument articulately and logically if you do not understand the argument in the first place. Second, it enables you to learn more about speech as you observe other speakers and use them as models. Finally, other speakers will inevitably have different interests and areas of expertise than you. By listening carefully to their speeches, you can learn about a wide variety of interesting subjects.

A poem written by an anonymous author summarizes the importance of listening best. It is applicable to speech class as to any situation.

> His thoughts were slow;
> His words were few
> And never formed to glisten,
> But he was joy
> To all his friends,
> You should of heard him listen.

BUILDING LISTENING SKILLS

You may be wondering, "Why do I have to learn to listen? After all, I do it all the time and I took this class to learn to speak." This is a common reaction of beginning speech students when they are asked to learn listening skills. However, these students forget that speaking is only part of the communciation process and that unless someone is listening, communication does not occur. Cristina Stuart, author of *How to Be an Effective Speaker*, relates this situation to throwing a baseball at a dart board. You may make a great throw and hit the bull's eye, but you have not accomplished the purpose of the game. If you can speak well but do not know how to listen — *really* listen — then you do not really understand the art of speaking.

Also, learning how to listen critically to others helps you improve as a speaker. Rudolph Verderber, author of *The Challenge of Effective Speaking*, claims that improving your listening helps you improve as a speaker because you are able to learn more about effective speech making, become a better critic of other speakers, and learn about a great number of subjects. In short, to be a good speaker, you need to be an effective listener.

Before learning how to do so, however, you need to know the definition of listening and, more importantly, critical listening. According to Joseph A. DeVito, listening is "the active process of receiving, processing, and retaining aural stimuli." Note that he says it is an "active" process. This means that the listener has a job to do other than simply hearing the speaker's words. DeVito defines critical listening as "the process of listening to a speech in order to render some kind of judgment or evaluation." Again, listeners have a job to do. They do not simply sit and stare at the speaker with vacant looks on their faces.

Barriers to Effective Listening

A number of factors keep us from listening as carefully and critically as we should. It is important to be aware of these in order to correct them and listen well.

1. **We become distracted.** External distractions, such as noises from outside the room, and internal distractions, such as hunger and fatigue, keep us from paying attention to a speaker.

2. **We may not understand a message.** At times, we may hear what is being said but do not understand the message.

3. **We have prejudices.** Because of our attitudes, we may not listen to certain messages or may not listen objectively.

4. **We forget messages over time.** Even if we hear a message and understand it, we may forget it as time passes.

5. **We often hear poor speakers.** Let's face it: some speakers are boring. They may have a dull voice, irritating mannerisms, or a poorly constructed speech. Often, we allow our minds to wander rather than listen to this type of speaker.

Improving Listening Skills

Despite the many problems that often make it very difficult to listen effectively, it is possible to learn to improve listening skills. You'll be surprised if you follow these suggestions how much you will improve as a speaker, and how much more you will enjoy listening. Quite simply, you need to become an active listener. As a general rule of thumb, people who are active are busier and consequently less bored. There are five basic suggestions that can help make you an effective critical listener.

1. **Prepare yourself to listen.** Have a positive attitude about listening to speeches. Tell yourself, "If I listen, I may learn something," rather than, "I'm probably going to be

41

bored by this speaker." Be willing to expend energy. To listen well, you need to be awake and alert, giving your full attention to the speaker. Finally, don't fake attention. We have all done this. For instance, say you are in class. Instead of listening to the instructor, you let your mind wander and daydream about the coming weekend. However, you still make eye contact with the instructor and may even nod if he looks at you. This is dangerous because you may miss important information and could be embarrassed if the speaker should ask you a question. It is much better to really listen than to simply pretend to listen.

2. ***Don't let your prejudices affect your ability to listen critically and impartially.*** This is another trap into which we have all fallen. Have you ever dismissed a speaker by saying, "He looks stupid," or "This is a boring topic"? Do not tune out a speaker simply because you do not like his appearance, choice of clothing, choice of topic, or you do not agree with his basic philosophies. You may miss something important.

3. ***Listen analytically.*** Try to go a step beyond simply *understanding* the speaker to *critiquing* the message. Try to identify the main ideas of the speech. Evaluate the logic being used. Search for any fallacy or faulty thinking. Evaluate the support materials (research, stories, examples, statistics) to determine how relevant they are to the speaker's thesis. You'll find that if you evaluate the speaker as you listen, you'll not only understand the message better, but will also remember it better later (something that could come in handy if the speaker happens to be a teacher and you will be tested on the material!).

4. ***Don't block out unpleasant messages.*** If you have strong feelings on a certain topic, such as taxes, political parties, abortion, or religion, there is a natural tendency to block out messages that are unpleasant to hear. However, this tendency prevents us from learning new information and

keeps us from learning about anything that is not consistent with our belief systems.

5. ***Take notes.*** Even if you are not in a class that requires you to remember certain information for an exam, note taking can help you maintain attention and prevent your mind from wandering. Many people find that, even if they never look at their notes after hearing a speaker, they remember the message better if they took notes while they were listening.

In summary, critical listening is an important skill to learn because it can help you become a better speaker, keep you from becoming bored, and help you learn about a variety of subjects. If you are a student, effective listening is essential to your success in school. By understanding the factors that prevent us from listening as well as we might and by being aware of techniques to improve listening skills, it is possible to improve this skill and go from simply hearing to really listening.

CLASSROOM ACTIVITIES

Individual and Group Activities Designed to Help Speakers Learn and Practice the Skills of Critical Listening

OBJECTIVES

Students will analyze their ability to listen critically to other speakers and practice the skills that will allow them to improve their listening ability.

Telephone Game

This is an old standby often used in classrooms and by speakers. An individual begins a message two to three sentences long by whispering it to a person in one corner of the room. That person then whispers it to the next individual and so on until everyone in the room has heard and passed on the message. After the message is given to the last person, that individual then repeats what he or she was told. Almost invariably, the message has been greatly altered by the time it is passed from student to student through the entire class.

This game illustrates how we don't often hear, process, and relay information correctly and can therefore demonstrate the need for improvement in listening skills.

Word Repetition Exercises

In this exercise, the teacher gives a series of words that, while they are actual English words, have no meaning in relation to each other. You must then repeat the series perfectly. If you do, one word is added to the list. This continues until you are no longer able to repeat all the words in the list without error. This activity can be made into a contest, with the student who is able to progress the longest declared the winner.

Another way to play this game is to choose partners. Each partner gets a different list of words and the two of

44

you go through the exercise together, keeping track of how far your partner is able to progress.

Student Analysis of Listening Skills

On the next page, you will find a test of listening skills modeled after similar exercises published by Verderber and DeVito. The purpose of this exercise is to measure your ability to listen effectively, determining your strengths and areas of needed improvement. It is important that you answer the questions honestly. Obviously, all the statements listed in the test are characteristic of effective listening. Therefore, higher scores indicate better critical listening skills. The test is printed on a separate sheet so that it may be copied and used again at different stages in the class.

Test Your Listening Skills

The following exercise is designed to give you an opportunity to measure your ability to listen critically to messages and determine your areas of strength and needed improvement in regard to your ability to listen.

Respond to each statement with the following scale: 5 = always; 4 = frequently; 3 = sometimes; 2 = seldom; 1 = never. Please answer all questions honestly and accurately — this exercise is designed to help you.

_____ 1. I listen differently for enjoyment, understanding, and evaluation.

_____ 2. When I listen to a speaker, I am able to distinguish between the main points and the supporting arguments.

_____ 3. When I am listening to gain information or to evaluate a speaker, I take good notes of the speech.

_____ 4. I listen to a speaker even if I am not initially impressed with his or her appearance or manner.

_____ 5. I listen to a speaker and evaluate the speech fairly even if he or she is stating views that contradict my own views.

_____ 6. If the subject matter of a speech is boring to me, I attempt to listen carefully rather than allowing my mind to wander.

_____ 7. I tend to focus more on the content of a speech than the delivery style of the speaker.

_____ 8. If I have to respond to a speaker or speak next, I still attempt to focus on the speech rather than planning what I will say.

_____ 9. If I critique a speech, I try to point out the good as well as the bad qualities of the speaker.

_____ 10. I try to listen to speakers I do not know as carefully as I would listen to a friend speak.

ASSIGNMENTS

An Explanation of the Objectives and Purposes of the Assignments Designed to Support the Material Teaching Effective Critical Listening Skills

Heckling Speech

The heckling speech is a fun exercise because it forces students to think on their feet by defending their assertions and requires that they become experts on a subject so that they will have the knowledge to answer any question on that subject. Additionally, it is more interesting for the audience as they are able to assume an active role in the speeches of their classmates and are forced to listen carefully to all speeches.

This assignment requires you to deliver a persuasive speech as that mode of speaking lends itself well to debate and questioning. However, it could be modified to fit any type of speech. Also, you will note that, in the model assignment, you will be required to ask questions as part of your grade. This insures that questions will be asked of the speakers and that all members of the class will remain actively involved.

The heckling speech is an effective speech to perform immediately before beginning any type of debate, as the skills learned here are prerequisite to the skills necessary for the refutation and rebuttal of arguments.

OBJECTIVES

1. To encourage you to listen carefully and critically to the speeches of your classmates by requiring you to ask questions regarding the content of the speeches.

2. To allow you to practice the skills of critical listening.

3. To introduce you to the skills of refutation by allowing you to ask critical questions about the content of messages to which you are exposed.

Student Evaluation Form

Evaluating other speakers is an invaluable activity for both beginning and advanced speakers for many reasons. First, it provides more incentive to listen carefully to speeches which makes the experience of listening more interesting and worthwhile. Also, speakers receive far more feedback on their performances than the instructor alone can provide when they are critiqued by an entire class. Finally, by evaluating others, speakers become more aware of their own strengths and weaknesses.

You will find a sample evaluation form on page 51 followed by a guide to evaluation. These should be used together as the guide provides suggestions and guidelines for the use of the evaluation form. The evaluation form is printed on a separate page so that copies may be made for each speech to be evaluated.

OBJECTIVES

1. To develop critical listening and evaluation skills.

2. To make you more aware of the principles of effective speech-making in regard to both content and delivery.

3. To help you learn to evaluate yourself as a speaker more critically through the practice gained by evaluating other speakers.

ASSIGNMENT
Heckling Speech

Assignment

You must deliver a persuasive speech on any issue that is controversial in nature. It is your job to persuade the audience to feel the same way about the issue as you. As you speak, you may be interrupted up to three times by the instructor or your classmates asking questions about the content of your speech. It is your responsibility to interrupt your speech and answer the questions to the best of your ability before moving on. Your grade will depend in part on the quality of your answers. Thus, to do well in this assignment, you must become an expert on your topic so that you will be prepared to answer any question you might face.

Topic Ideas

Any issue that is controversial may be selected. Areas you could draw from include current issues, social issues, or school and community issues. However, it must be a topic that has two sides and can be debated.

Heckling Questions

1. Everyone must ask questions of at least five speakers. Any member of the class who does not do so will not fulfill the requirements of the assignment and will lose points on their grade.

2. To be recognized by the speaker, you must stand. The speaker will then call on you and you may then ask your question.

3. Questions may ask the speaker to clarify a point made in the speech, require the speaker to defend a point made, or go beyond the speech by requiring information on the topic not provided by the speaker.

4. All questions should be asked in a polite, courteous manner.

5. You are not allowed to argue with the speaker. You may only interrupt if you have a question!

Other Requirements

TIME: 3 to 5 minutes, not counting time spent answering questions

DUE DATE:

Student Evaluation Form

Using this form, please evaluate speeches in the areas listed. You may use the questions on the evaluation guide to direct your observation and criticism. Please be critical, but also be positive and constructive.

Speaker: _____   Evaluator: _____

Subject and Purpose

Content

Introduction

Body

Conclusion

Overall

Delivery

Student Evaluation Guide

As you evaluate speeches, use the following questions as a guide to direct your observation and criticism.

Subject and Purpose

Is the subject worthwhile?

Is the subject relevant and interesting to the audience?

Does the speaker seem to be an expert on the subject?

Does the speaker accomplish the general purpose of the assignment (to inform, persuade, entertain, etc.)?

Content

Is the speech adequately researched?
Are the sources credible? That is, are they reliable and up to date?

Introduction

Does the speaker gain your attention?

Is the thesis clearly stated?

Are the main ideas of the speech made clear?

Body

Is the speech well organized? Do ideas flow smoothly from one to another?

Are the main points related to the thesis?

Are transitions between main points clear?

Is each assertion adequately supported through examples, research, evidence, etc.?

Is the language used appropriate for the purpose and style of the speech?

Are grammatical errors made?

Conclusion

Does the speaker restate the thesis and main ideas?

Is the ending powerful? Does it leave you thinking about the speech even after it is over?

Delivery

Does the speaker maintain eye contact with the audience?

Does the speaker have any mannerisms that distract from the speech (such as swaying, fidgeting, etc.)?

Can the speaker easily be heard?

Does the speaker use an appropriate amount of vocal expression and inflection?

Are the rate and volume appropriate?

Does the speaker effectively use gestures and expressions that add power and meaning to the speech?

Topic Selection, Organization, and Research

Choosing a Dynamic Topic, Organizing
a Speech, and Effectively Using Research

Introduction

This chapter deals with three topics that are among the hardest stages in speech preparation, but also among the most important elements in determining the success of a speech. These topics are methods and criteria for topic selection, effective speech organization, and research techniques. Perhaps these topics are difficult because they are simply not exciting. In the process of speech preparation, many speakers look forward to these tasks the least. This chapter attempts to help with this problem by providing activities as well as an assignment that requires the use of these difficult but essential skills.

You'll note that in the instructional essay, a section is provided on alternatives to traditional outlines. These suggestions have often proven invaluable to students who do not process in a linear fashion, giving them an aid for organization not just of speeches, but also of essays, reports, and any other writing they may be called on to produce. It should be emphasized that these suggestions do not excuse speakers from meeting all the criteria of organization, but merely give them another means by which they may visualize an outline.

Though difficult, the topics discussed in this chapter deserve a great amount of attention. The selection of the topic is the first key in gaining the attention of the audience. The organization of the speech provides a foundation for the content; without it, the entire speech becomes incomprehensible. Likewise, the use of research and evidence are a foundation for the support and proof of assertions made in a speech.

TOPIC SELECTION

If you've ever watched the television news, you know that before every commercial, the newscasters tell the audience what stories will be featured when they return. We all know why they do this: they hope that the topics of the stories will be interesting enough to keep their viewers from turning the channel during the commercials. Often, this works. You can also entice your audience to listen to your speech if the topic you choose is of interest to them. However, you can turn your audience off at the very beginning of your speech if you choose a topic that is not of interest to them, not relevant to them, or if it is a subject they feel they have heard too much about. Because of this, the selection of topic is one of the most important elements in speech preparation.

Guidelines for Selecting a Speech Topic

1. *Choose a topic you care about.* If you don't care about your topic, you are likely to be bored speaking on it. What will this do to your audience? However, if you really care about your topic, this will be contagious and your audience will also care. Also, it will be easier for you to speak.

2. *Choose a topic you know a great deal about (or care to learn about).* In order to speak well on a subject, you need to be an expert on it. Therefore, choose a topic on which you have a great deal of knowledge or wouldn't mind taking the time to study.

3. *Choose a topic that is interesting to the audience.* No matter how much you enjoy a certain topic, your speech will not reach anyone if your audience isn't also interested. Analyze your audience. Determine what types of topics would interest them based on their average age, socioeconomic situation, geographic conditions, etc. If you can, ask a few members of your audience to see what they think of possible choices.

4. *Choose topics that are original.* Some topics, no matter

how important or relevant, become boring when an audience has simply heard too much information on them. If you do use a topic that may be over-discussed, try to find a unique approach to present it. One student, speaking on the common theme of labeling and stereotyping people, made humorous observations about labels on products to show the dangers of labeling people.

How to Find Topics

1. *Brainstorm.* Without evaluating them, make a list of as many topics as possible.

2. *"Browse" in the library.* Go to the library, not to research for a specific topic, but to browse for topic ideas. Look at current magazines and the index to magazine articles. Browse the nonfiction shelves in areas that interest you.

3. *Read.* Keep up on the news. Read newspapers, magazines, as well as books. The more you know, the more ideas you will have.

4. *Ask for ideas.* Often, other people will come up with ideas you may not have on your own.

ORGANIZING A SPEECH

It is *very* important that you structure and organize your speech. Studies have shown that people who hear speeches that are structured are more likely to understand, remember, and be persuaded by the message compared to people who hear the exact same material without structure. An excellent means of providing structure to a speech is called the Tell-Tell-Tell Structure. Using this means of organization, you tell your audience what you're going to tell them, proceed to tell them, then tell them what you told them. While this may seem repetitive, it is really very necessary. Have you ever been reading a textbook and realized that your eyes had scanned two or three pages, but you had no idea what was said? When this happens while reading, we can simply turn back a few pages and reread. However, if your mind wanders while listening to a speech, you cannot ask the speaker to repeat the last couple minutes of his speech. Therefore, it is important for you, as a speaker, to provide a structure for your audience to follow so that they don't get lost during your speech. All speeches should have three parts: the introduction, body, and conclusion.

The Introduction

The introduction should accomplish three purposes: to get the attention of the audience, to state the thesis of the speech, and to preview the main points that will be used in the speech.

1. ***Get the attention of the audience.*** The very first thing you need to do is to draw the audience into your topic, to make them interested in what you have to say. This can be done in many ways: a startling statement, a rhetorical question, an interesting story or anecdote, a quotation, a humorous observation or story, a startling statistic, etc. No matter which technique is chosen, be sure it deals with the subject of the speech and effectively draws the audience into the speech.

2. ***State the thesis of the speech.*** The *topic* is the subject of the speech. The *thesis* is the speaker's specific stance on the topic. It is the goal of the speech, the main point, the most important idea the speaker will prove. After gaining the attention of the audience, state very clearly exactly what it is you hope to prove in your speech.

3. ***Preview your main points (give a roadmap).*** This is the first "Tell" in the Tell-Tell-Tell Structure. By briefly stating the main points that will be used to support the thesis, you focus your information for your audience. Think of it this way: when you begin a trip, what is the first thing you do? If you've never made the trip before, you will look at a map to get a general idea of where you are

going. The preview of points serves as a roadmap for the audience by giving them a plan of the journey you will take them on during your speech.

The Conclusion

People like to have a sense of completion. Have you ever heard part of a song, but had to turn it off in the middle? It is very likely when this has happened that you either felt annoyed or continued to hum the song on your own. This is because you did not feel a sense of conclusion, or completeness. When you are speaking, your audience also needs to feel as if you've brought your speech to an adequate conclusion. Clark S. Carlile and Dana Hensley, authors of *38 Basic Speech Experiences*, liken a conclusion to a sunset in that, as a sunset signals the end of a day, the conclusion signals the end of a speech. They say, "The conclusion brings together all the thoughts, emotions, discussions, arguments, and feelings which the speaker has tried to communicate to the audience."

Like the introduction, the conclusion should accomplish three purposes: it should restate the thesis, summarize the main points, and signal the speech's end.

1. *Restate the thesis.* Since the thesis is your main idea, the one thing you want your audience to believe, you need to use every opportunity to reinforce this idea in their minds.

2. *Summarize main points.* Now that you've come to the end of the "journey," tell the audience where they've been. This is the third "Tell" in Tell-Tell-Tell.

3. *Signal the end of the speech (end with a bang!).* The final thing to do in a speech is to let the audience know you've come to the end and to keep them thinking about your thesis after they leave and perhaps even do something about the problem you've noted. You can use any attention-getting technique to accomplish this or even

directly call the audience to action.

The Body

The body is the meat of your speech, the part that includes your major arguments and support for your thesis. Some suggestions for writing:

1. *Use main points.* To structure your speech, you need to break your arguments into general main ideas. Use two to four points so that you will have enough to develop your thesis but few enough so that the audience can remember them all. Each main point should develop and support your thesis and should be restricted to a single idea. Remember: a main point is not a supporting fact, but rather a general assertion that can be supported by facts.

2. *Organize your main points in a logical structure.* To help your audience follow your speech, you should organize your points in a logical manner. Some ways you can do this:

    Chronological or Time Order. This means to organize your points in an order that follows the sequence of a series of events. For instance, you could look at a problem in the past, the present, and the future.

    Spatial Order. In spatial order, you organize your points in the way they relate to each other in space. For instance, you could look at the problem of pollution in the United States by considering the different types of pollution in the Northeast, the South, and the West.

    Inductive Order. Inductive reasoning moves from specific to general. The speaker begins with specific facts and gradually builds to a general conclusion (the thesis).

    Deductive Order. This is the opposite of inductive reasoning. The speaker begins by making a broad, general assertion and then supporting it with specific facts.

Remember, deductive sounds like detective. A detective begins with a general fact (someone has been murdered, for example) and then must learn the specifics (who did it, what was the means, what was the motive, etc.)

3. *Provide transitions between main points.* Remember our analogy of how a preview of points serves as a roadmap because it tells the audience where you will journey on your speech. Following the same line of reasoning, transitions are like signs. Even if you have a map, you will have a very difficult time following it if the roads on your trip have no signs alerting you where to exit and informing you of which road you are on. As signs guide you on a trip, transitions tell the audience exactly where you are on the journey of the speech. According to Hamilton Gregory, "[Transitions are] a way of saying, 'I've finished Thought A; now I'm going to Thought B.' " Simple phrases like, "Let's go to my second point," and "This brings us to my third main idea" can serve as transitions.

The Outline

When you put all these elements of a speech together, you will have an outline that looks something like this:

I. Introduction
   A. Attention-getter
   B. Statement of Thesis
   C. Preview of Main Points

II. Body
   A. Point A
      1. Transition to point
      2. Statement of the point
      3. Explanation of the point being made
      4. Evidence and support
      5. Explanation of relation of evidence and point
   B. Point B
      (repeat 1-5)

C. Point C
   (repeat 1-5)

III. Conclusion
   A. Restatement of Thesis
   B. Summary of Points
   C. Signal of the end of the Speech

Alternatives to Traditional Outlines

As much as some teachers would like all students to use traditional outlines like the one above, the reality is that not everyone sees the world in such an organized, linear fashion. For some people, outlines make perfect sense and are very easy to create. However, other people struggle when forced to design an outline. This does not mean they are less intelligent than the outline-capable, but rather that they have a different way of understanding things. The following are alternatives suggested by Ron Hoff for those who are not good with outlines. Remember, the speech still needs to have an introduction, body, and conclusion. These are just alternatives for picturing those components for speakers.

1. ***Think of your speech as a game board.*** Place your main points on a board of a game such as "Monopoly" or "Candyland." As your piece would move around the game board, you will follow the same pattern to place your points and supporting arguments. For instance, if a "Monopoly" game were used, the main points could be placed in the corner spots and the supporting arguments in between.

2. ***Think of your speech as following a pathway or a route.*** You could place your points on a map, or create your own route. If you choose, you can use arrows, big blocky letters, etc. Use whatever works for you.

3. ***Draw your own graphics to help you visualize and remember the main components of your presentation.*** Rather than outlining with words, you can outline with

pictures. It doesn't matter if anyone else can identify or recognize anything you've drawn so long as it helps you remember your outline.

4. ***Use your visual aids to help you remember the main points and ideas.*** Hoff provides an example of a speaker who gave a presentation to an organization on how to communicate more effectively with direct mail. He brought in, as a visual aid, a mailbox with a number of letters inside. Each letter represented a different point in his speech. As the speaker pulled each letter out of the box, he was able to remember his next point and also provided the audience with something concrete to help them remember his presentation.

USING RESEARCH IN A SPEECH

Before you present, you need to hit the library and find all the information you can on your topic. This serves two purposes: first, it allows you to become an "expert" on the subject before you speak on it; second, it gives you evidence to use in your speech for proof and for credibility. Simply, your audience is more likely to listen to your speech and believe you if it's clear that you've done your homework. No one wants to listen to a speaker who doesn't know what he's talking about.

Where to Find Evidence

You know you need to research your topic, so you've gone to the obvious place: the library. Now, as you look at the stacks of books, magazines, encyclopedias, and other materials, you wonder, "Where do I begin?" What follows is a list of the best places to research in the library.

1. ***Periodicals.*** Periodicals, or magazines, are probably the best source of information because they are brief and provide the most recent information on a subject. If your library has a computerized index to magazines, this will

greatly speed the time it takes you to find articles on your topic.

2. **Newsbank.** This is a source of recent newspaper articles on a subject and provides the same advantages as a magazine index.

3. **SIRS Files.** Many libraries have SIRS files, which are an accumulated collection of articles grouped by topic. This is a very easy source to use if your library has it.

4. **Books and Texts.** To find appropriate books and texts, use the card catalog or computerized index, depending on which your library has. The danger with using books for sources is that there is often too much information to sift through quickly and they are sometimes outdated.

5. **Books of Quotations.** If appropriate, a quotation can add support and interest to your speech.

6. **Resource Materials.** Texts such as encyclopedias, biographical sources, atlases, and almanacs can provide facts and statistics on almost any subject.

7. **Interview.** In addition to researching in the library, it can also be of great benefit to a speaker to interview people who have special knowledge of a certain issue or topic. For instance, if a speaker has chosen "The Horrors of War" as a topic, interviews with military veterans could add much to the speech.

How to Use Research and Supporting Materials in Your Speech

1. *Support all assertions in a speech.* Everything you say should be proven in your speech. You can do this through logical reasoning, the use of relevant stories and examples, or through reference to research.

2. *Use credible, reputable sources.* We've all seen headlines on supermarket tabloids such as "Mother Gives

Birth to Two-Headed Baby" and thought little of them. That's because these tabloids have a reputation for fabricating ridiculous stories. However, if we saw the same headline in a newspaper with a good reputation, we'd be more likely to take notice. When selecting materials to use for support, be sure to use sources that have high credibility with your audience.

3. *Evidence may be either directly quoted or paraphrased.* However, whenever you use words or ideas that are not your own, you need to give credit to the source or you will be guilty of plagiarism.

4. *When evidence is used, a source citation should be given.* At the very least, provide the name of the author and the source (title of the book or magazine) from which the evidence is taken. In more formal speeches, also include the title of the article, if applicable, and the publishing date of the source.

Admittedly, selecting a topic, organizing, and researching speeches are not the most exciting or enjoyable parts of speech preparation. However, they are essential to any speaker who wishes to present a coherent, well structured, believable speech. If you take the time to properly complete these three steps of preparation, you'll find that your audience will be more likely to listen to you, understand your speech, remember what you have said, and, perhaps most importantly, believe you.

CLASSROOM ACTIVITIES
Individual and Group Activities
to Provide Practice in the Principles
of Speech Organization and Research Methods

OBJECTIVES

To provide opportunities for practice of the principles of speech organization and research methods.

Attention-Getting Contest

The instructor will select a speech topic and narrow it to a specific thesis. Write an attention-getter for a speech on the topic. This need not be an entire introduction, but only the first fifteen to thirty seconds of a speech that attempts to "grab" the audience. Next, deliver your grabber. After everyone has presented, a vote can be conducted to determine which student's device was most effective at drawing the audience into the speech and focusing their attention on the topic. The class may choose to offer a reward for the student who finishes with the most votes.

Organizational Maze

Melody Huffman of Amber University in Texas suggests using what she calls a "maze" to help you make an outline. Write down answers to the questions below. By doing so, you are essentially forming an outline to a speech on your given topic.

1. What is your topic?

2. Below this, write down exactly what you wish to say about your topic. What is your main idea, or thesis?

3. What are three or four arguments or points that could help you prove your thesis? That is, what are some reasons you can use to prove your thesis true? These are your main points.

4. For each main point, list at least two facts or pieces of reasoning that support them and help prove them true. These will be your supporting arguments.

Huffman asserts that by breaking the process of organizing ideas down into separate individual steps, the idea of providing structure to a speech seems less daunting and can greatly help with speech organization.

Practice Visual Map

Choose a topic on which you would like to speak. Next, come up with a thesis for your topic as well as three main points supporting your thesis. Then draw a visual outline as described in the "Alternatives to Outlines" section of the instructional essay. Be as creative and innovative as possible in translating your outline to visual form. When everyone has completed their visual guides, present them to the class. Explain what yours means and how it could help you, as a speaker, remember your outline.

This activity not only affords the opportunity to practice creating a visual outline, but also, through the process of seeing what others have drawn, allows you to see a number of possibilities of what can be done with this application.

Library Scavenger Hunt

Break into teams of two to four. The instructor will give each group a list of materials, facts, and information that can be found in the library. As quickly as possible, find all the materials on your list. The winning group will be the first group to find all the materials. This game can help you find your way around a library as it requires you to consult a wide variety of sources.

ASSIGNMENT

An Explanation of the Objectives and Purposes of the Assignment Designed to Support the Material Teaching the Principles of Topic Selection, Speech Organization, and Research Methods

Current Event Speech

The current event speech is included in this chapter because it provides a very easy assignment through which the skills of speech organization and research can be practiced. Because the main points of the speech are prescribed, it helps students divide their speeches into different points and makes it easy to follow the outline provided in the instructional notes for effective speech organization with success. Also, because it is an assignment that is reliant upon research, this assignment provides experience in using outside sources for support in presentations. Finally, an additional advantage of this assignment is that, by presenting both sides of the issue, speakers are practicing an essential debate skill: the ability to anticipate and attack the probable arguments of their opponents.

OBJECTIVES

1. To teach the principles of effective speech organization and to provide an opportunity for the practice of said principles.

2. To provide experience in using outside sources and research for support in a speech.

Note

Though there is only one suggested assignment for this chapter, other assignments offered elsewhere also allow an opportunity to practice the objectives taught in this chapter. These assignments include the persuasive and informative speeches (Chapter Seven), as well as the oratory, or memorized speech (Chapter Six).

70

ASSIGNMENT
Current Event Speech

Assignment

Deliver a speech that examines a current issue that is important and controversial in our world today. It will be your job to explain the issue as well as the arguments supporting both sides of the controversy. You must choose an issue that could be debated and would have two opposing sides, or viewpoints. Your first main point will be one side of the issue, your second the opposing side, and your third main point will be *your* opinion and an explanation of the reasons you take that side.

Topic Ideas

You may choose any issue as long as it is timely and of importance today. Since the speech deals with current events, the best places to look for ideas are newspapers and news magazines, such as *Time, Newsweek,* and *U.S. News and World Report.* If you have a specific issue in mind, you will be able to find information on it at the library.

Below is a list of possible topics. As always, you are not restricted to this list.

1. Should the U.S. impose more strict restrictions concerning the possession and ownership of guns?

2. Does the KKK have the right to march in situations in which they might incite a riot?

3. How can the deficit best be reduced?

4. Does the American educational system need reform?

5. What can America do to help cure the drug crisis?

6. How can we best help the homeless?

7. Should professional sports leagues be tougher on athletes who use drugs?

71

8. Should the U.S. provide more money to help people in other countries who are less fortunate than us?

Other Requirements

You must speak from an outline and turn it in at the conclusion of your speech.

You must use at least one piece of research for support in your speech. You must give a full source citation of the evidence during the speech and turn a copy of it in at the conclusion of your speech.

TIME: 3 to 5 minutes

DUE DATE:

Different Modes of Speaking

Delivering Impromptu, Manuscript,
and Memorized Speeches

Introduction

In applied, real-world situations, individuals are often called upon to make speeches and presentations. However, the situation, tone, and formality of these speeches vary greatly. It is for this reason that you need to learn to use different methods of delivery, to prepare you for any speaking situation that you may encounter later in life. This chapter allows you to learn three different types of delivery: impromptu, speaking from a manuscript, and the delivery of memorized speeches. In essence, you will learn and practice the principles and skills of the type of speaking that allows for the least amount of preparation (impromptu) as well as the type of speaking that allows for the most preparation (memorized).

Randall Bytwerk of Calvin College, writing in *Communication Education*, states, "The impromptu speech, perhaps the type most often given, is also one of the most neglected in public speaking courses." He goes on to list five reasons it should be taught in public speaking courses:

1. The impromptu is a commonly delivered type of speech.

2. Impromptu speaking is not a skill developed by other regular speaking assignments.

3. Impromptu exercises teach other critical speaking skills.

4. Impromptu speeches are fun.

5. Impromptu speaking exercises afford a profitable way to use unexpected time at the end of a class period.

Clearly, there are many situations in which you will be required to speak in an impromptu manner. Job interviews, club, school, and business meetings, and class assignments are just a few. It is essential to learn the skills that will allow you to speak effectively in these situations.

Still, while impromptu speaking is an invaluable skill, it is often necessary for speakers to use a complete manuscript or to memorize a speech. Though an ever-increasing number of instructors and writers warn against these techniques, and with very good reasons, they are sometimes unavoidable. Often, speakers deliver messages that will be recorded or reprinted and must therefore be carefully phrased. The news media is one factor that causes many speeches to be either written or memorized. Gordon Zimmerman, author of *Public Speaking Today*, tells how, in the 1976 presidential primaries, Jimmy Carter stated that neighborhoods should retain "ethnic purity." This term suggested to some that Carter was justifying racism, and he was forced to apologize. Zimmerman concludes that "a carefully written manuscript would not have included [that phrase]." Also, there are other, more formal speaking situations, when a speaker will want to have an address carefully and completely prepared. For instance, if you give a commencement address or speak in front of your church, you might choose to use a manuscript or even memorize the address. Finally, competitive speech contests often require students to memorize entire speeches. Events such as oratory in high school forensics and informative, persuasive, and after-dinner speaking in collegiate forensics all require students to memorize eight- to ten-minute speeches word for word. Therefore, learning how to effectively prepare and deliver such a speech can be a great benefit to those who are interested in entering competitive speech contests.

The instructions in this chapter tell when it is best to use the various modes of speaking addressed, give the advantages and disadvantages of each, and provide suggestions for the preparation and delivery of speeches in each mode. The activities and assignments are opportunities to practice the skills discussed. You will note that there is no formal assignment provided requiring speaking from a manuscript. The reason for this is simple — a manuscript speech can be a speech of any type in which the speaker uses a script. Therefore, you may practice this type of speaking by using any other speech assignment, simply reading it from a manuscript.

THE IMPROMPTU STYLE OF SPEAKING

Mark Twain said, "It usually takes more than three weeks to prepare a good impromptu speech." You may wonder, "How can that be? After all, the point of impromptu is to speak with little or no preparation." True, in the impromptu mode of speaking, the speaker is called upon on the spur of the moment and must rely on remote preparation entirely due to the lack of time to outline or rehearse the speech. Still, if one is to be effective in this mode of speaking, it takes a great amount of know-how, practice, and thinking about possible speaking situations.

Because of the relative lack of time to prepare impromptu speeches, this mode of speaking often strikes fear in the hearts of beginning (and even advanced) speech students. This is natural. However, it is essential for all students to learn to speak well without a great deal of time to prepare. There are innumerable situations in which impromptu speaking is required. If you are called upon to answer a question in a class, in a job interview, or to debate your position in a community meeting, you will need to use impromptu speaking skills. Leon Fletcher, author of *How to Design and Deliver a Speech*, identifies two benefits of developing your skills as an impromptu speaker. First, as already mentioned, you'll be better able to present your ideas in class discussions, business meetings, professional conferences, as well as club and organizational meetings. Second, building your skills as an impromptu speaker will help you develop ability and confidence in all speaking situations. Therefore, since impromptu speaking is so valuable, you need to learn to do it correctly.

Suggestions for Effective Delivery of Impromptu Speeches

1. ***Prepare to speak.*** Even though impromptu seems like something for which you can't prepare, nothing could be farther from the truth. There is perhaps no other type of

speaking where practice and preparation are as essential to a speaker's success. Carol Marrs says, "Practice is the way to master the impromptu method of speaking." It often helps to anticipate situations in which you may be called upon to speak and questions you may be asked. This allows you to practice speeches on specific topics that are probably close to topics you may really face. Another way to prepare yourself to speak effectively in an impromptu manner is to read often and remember interesting jokes, anecdotes, and facts that you discover. If you have information at the ready, you can often incorporate it into your speeches.

2. ***Choose your topic quickly and wisely.*** If you are given a choice of more than one subject on which you may speak, make your decision as quickly as possible. Often, in classroom situations, students are given a choice of two or three different topics. When this happens, you don't want to waste any of your valuable preparation time choosing a topic, so pick one quickly and stick with it. Carlile and Hensley offer one primary rule to help you select a topic: choose the topic on which you are best fitted to speak. You should also consider your audience and the occasion.

3. ***Organize your speech.*** Follow the same pattern of organization you would for any other speech. Be sure to include an introduction that gets the attention of your audience, states your topic or the question you have been asked, and previews the main points, or ideas, of your speech. Break the body of your speech into two or three main points. Finally, provide a conclusion that restates the thesis of your speech, summarizes your points, and has a strong concluding statement. If you make as much of an outline as your preparation time allows, your speech will be coherent, focused, and will have a greater chance of being well developed. However, if you don't provide some sort of organization, your speech is very likely to wander and meander, making no specific point. Also, impromptu

speakers who don't organize often run out of things to say long before those with outlines and end up giving very short speeches.

4. ***Make a blank outline before speaking.*** If you know that you will be required to give an impromptu speech and will be allowed to create brief notes, it can be beneficial to make a blank outline. That is, write down what you want to remember to include in your introduction and conclusion and leave space for at least three main points. This saves you time during the brief preparation of the speech and reminds you to organize your ideas into an outline.

5. ***Use preset patterns of organization.*** Often, if you have several patterns or orders by which you can organize your speech in mind, you can apply one to the question you are asked. These patterns include the two-sided argument, in which you present both sides of an issue and determine which is most valid; chronological order, which looks at an issue in terms of the past, present, and future; space order, which looks at issues by area, or region; causal order, which discusses certain forces and then points out the results of those forces; and the motivational sequence, which shows a need, provides a plan, then demonstrates how that plan will solve for the need. For instance, if your are asked to speak on the question "Is censorship justified in certain situations?", you could break it down into a two-sided argument, considering first reasons justifying certain forms of censorship, then stating the point of view that asserts censorship is never justified, and finally discussing which point of view you believe has the most merit.

6. ***Stick to your outline.*** In an impromptu speech, there is often a tendency among speakers to leave the outline, either getting off the subject or rambling on about the subject without actually saying anything new. This is

because when speakers have little time to prepare, new thoughts and ideas will invariably come to mind during their speeches. Try to avoid this tendency. Stick to your outline, incorporating new ideas only if they fit in with your original pattern of organization. If you try to change patterns of organization in the middle of a speech, you will confuse your audience and probably yourself.

THE MANUSCRIPT STYLE OF SPEAKING

Manuscript speaking involves word-for-word reading of a prepared text, with little or no deviation from the planned wording. This type of speaking holds many advantages for the speaker. First, since the wording of the speech is carefully prepared and thought out, the speech can be delivered without the possibility of errors in the stating of important information. Poor phrasing or lapses of memory are not a concern when a manuscript is used. Second, the use of a manuscript can calm a speaker's nerves, as little is left to chance during the presentation. Finally, the use of a manuscript can assure that a speech will be within time limits. Speakers who must deliver messages that need to be an exact time, such as radio and television broadcasters, are often required to use a manuscript.

However, there are also many disadvantages in using a manuscript to deliver a speech, so many that most researchers and instructors in the field now recommend against it. When a manuscript is used, the amount of eye contact speakers can make with the audience is limited, and interaction with the audience is decreased. Also, speakers are confined by manuscripts and will typically use fewer gestures and less movement during their presentations. Next, the preparation of a manuscript can be a very time-consuming task. People who must speak frequently cannot afford to devote the necessary time to manuscript preparation. Finally, speakers using manuscripts are less able to spontaneously adapt to their audiences.

Still, if you must use a manuscript in the presentation of your speech, there are many things you can do to make your presentation as effective as possible.

Suggestions for Effective Delivery of Manuscript Speeches

1. *Make sure your speech is as well written as possible.* Since you can completely prepare the content of your speech ahead of time, make sure you take the time to check your wording, grammar, and the development of your ideas.

2. *Use a typed manuscript.* Use a fairly large-size print, double or triple space, and make clear divisions or notations at main points. Since all of these things increase the readability of a script, they reduce the chance for error during a presentation.

3. *Check pronunciation of all words you have difficulty pronouncing.*

4. *Make marks on the manuscript.* Another advantage of a manuscript is that you have a place to remind yourself of techniques you want to use in your presentation. Note on the manuscript where you want to pause, use special emphasis, speed up, or slow down. Also, make sure the page breaks are at the end of paragraphs or sentences to avoid awkward pauses and interruptions during the speech.

5. *Number your pages.* This prevents them from getting out of order before you speak, which leaves you searching for the correct sheet in the middle of the speech. Though it can be quite entertaining for the audience to watch a speaker flip through all of his or her sheets in the middle of a presentation muttering things like "I know it's here somewhere," speakers do not generally enjoy this experience.

6. *Practice with your script.* Frequently, sentence wording will not sound natural and should be altered before the presentation. Practice reading the script as naturally as it would be spoken in conversation. Also, work on "reading ahead" so that you can see what's next on the script and then look up and make eye contact with the audience while you are speaking.

7. *Be willing to deviate from the script.* If the audience clearly does not understand a point, be willing to elaborate or provide additional examples. If their feedback is negative, you should leave the script and use techniques, such as humor, to try to reinvolve them.

THE MEMORIZED MODE OF SPEAKING

The memorized mode of speaking is just that: the delivery of a speech that has been carefully written, scripted, and then memorized word for word. Like manuscript speaking, it is rarely recommended that you completely memorize a speech. However, it is sometimes desirable or even necessary. The memorized mode of speaking has the same advantages and benefits as the manuscript mode. Preparation time is great, and the speech can be carefully planned and worded. Because every aspect of a memorized speech can be planned and practiced, speeches in this mode that are done well can be quite powerful. The advantage of memorized over manuscript speeches is that the speakers are more free to move around and use their bodies to enhance delivery.

However, memorized and manuscript speeches also share most of the same disadvantages. The delivery style can seem unnatural and speeches are not spontaneous or open to audience feedback. Also, when a speech is memorized, speakers create the possibility of forgetting their lines during the speech, leaving a long, awkward pause. Still, there is a time and a place for memorized speeches. Here you will be given suggestions to help you memorize a speech as well as to deliver a memorized speech.

Suggestions for the
Memorization of a Speech

When students are asked to memorize a speech, they often panic, and probably with good reason. This can be a difficult, time-consuming, and daunting task. However, if a speech is to be memorized, it must be memorized perfectly to prevent embarrassing lapses of memory. There are many techniques to aid in the process of memorization. None are guaranteed to work for everyone, so find those that work for you and use them.

1. *Memorize line by line.* Repeat the first line of your speech until you have it down perfectly, then do the same with the second. Next, put the two together and repeat them until you know them cold. Add the third line. Continue until you have the first paragraph. Then do the second paragraph, then put the two together. Add another, and another, until the entire speech is completed.

2. *Tape your speech on cassette.* Listen to the tape while jogging, working, driving, studying, or any other time you might listen to music. This will help reinforce it in your mind.

3. *Type your speech.* It is often easier to memorize a script that is neat and clean.

4. *Memorize before going to sleep.* It has been suggested that we remember things we learn immediately before bed best. So if memorization is the last thing you do before falling asleep, you might have a better chance of remembering it. Perhaps you'll even dream about your speech.

5. *Roll up your sleeves and do it!* This may sound like an advertisement for athletic shoes, but there is no substitute for plain hard work when it comes to memorization. So put some time and effort into it and get it done!

Suggestions for Effective Delivery of Memorized Speeches

1. ***Try to speak without a podium.*** Since you have no notes or manuscript when delivering a memorized speech, it is the perfect opportunity to step away from the comfort of the podium. This makes you more free to move, eliminates a barrier between you and the audience, and shows greater confidence and composure.

2. ***Use gestures.*** As with any speech, your gestures should add emphasis to the content of your speech. However, since you don't have notes in the memorized mode of speaking and may not use a podium, there is even more of a premium on the use of gestures in your speech. See Chapter Two for more detailed instructions on the use of gestures while speaking.

3. ***Use movement.*** Taking steps during a speech helps separate main points physically and makes you seem more conversational. Remember — move only between main ideas and only for a specific purpose. Don't allow your movement to become pacing.

4. ***Make direct eye contact with your audience.*** Again, this is absolutely essential in the memorized mode of speaking. Since you have no notes to look at, you should make constant eye contact with your audience.

There are many different situations in which speakers are called upon to speak. Some, like the impromptu mode, allow for very little or no preparation time. Others, like the manuscript and memorized modes, require extensive preparation. However, by being aware of when to use different types of speeches and by using effective techniques when speaking in these modes, speakers can show confidence and speak effectively no matter the specific demands of a situation.

CLASSROOM ACTIVITIES

Individual and Group Activities
to Help Develop Effective Techniques
for the Delivery of Speeches in Different Modes

OBJECTIVES

To provide experience for speakers using the impromptu, manuscript, and memorized modes of delivery.

Job Interview

Since the job interview is one of the most common and important real-life situations in which impromptu speaking skills are used, this activity provides essential practice.

Pick a specific job in a career field you are considering. Either the instructor or another student will act as the boss or personnel manager at the hiring firm and ask questions appropriate to the situation. You must answer the questions to the best of your ability, with the intention of being selected for the position.

Be sure to remember the importance of nonverbals, appearance, and manner in this particular speaking situation. Throughout the entire exercise, you should act exactly as you would in an actual job interview.

The Serial Speech

In this activity, one student begins a speech or story and speaks for thirty to forty seconds. The next student picks up where the first stopped. This continues until all students have had an opportunity to speak. These speeches usually take entertaining lines and provide you with an opportunity to think on your feet in a fun, nonthreatening situation.

The Two-Speaking-At-Once Contest

Two students speak simultaneously on the same topic

or different topics for thirty to sixty seconds. The class votes on whose presentation was more effective, and the winner moves to the next round. This process of elimination continues until one student is declared the overall winner. This activity is beneficial because it demonstrates the importance of delivery techniques, provides practice in impromptu speaking, forces you to project your voice and speak with greater energy, and is enjoyable as you focus on the competition and not your anxiety about the impromptu mode of speaking.

The Pet Peeve Speech

Identify the subject that angers you the most and then speak on why you are so bothered by that issue. You may even hit a table in front of you with a rolled up newspaper to vent your frustrations. If you have trouble displaying emotion and conviction in your delivery style, this is a good way to overcome your problem. Randall L. Bytwerk, author of an article on impromptu speaking exercises in *Communication Education*, asserts, "The most stubbornly monotonic speaker can display startling energy during this assignment."

The Sales Speech

The instructor will bring a bag filled with various objects such as an old gym sock, a wire whisk, an old spoon, or a used battery. You must draw an object out of the bag and then attempt to sell it to the class. For instance, if you draw a single used gym sock out of the bag you could sell it as an insect repellent.

The Desperate Plea

This exercise forces you to speak in a hypothetical situation. You will be given a desperate situation (your airplane has been hijacked by a terrorist group threatening to kill you and everyone else aboard unless you can persuade them to do otherwise; you are about to be expelled for excessive practical joking and must speak before a board of appeals) and must attempt to talk your way out of the situation. The class can play the role of the appropriate audience and determine your fate to make the exercise more interesting.

Soapbox Derby

This activity is beneficial as it provides an opportunity to practice impromptu skills as you get on a "soapbox" to give your opinion of certain issues. The instructor or a member of the class must serve as the moderator. The moderator begins the activity by stating an issue that is current, relevant, and debatable. Next, the moderator will ask more specific questions dealing with the issue and call on members of the class at random to answer those questions. If you are called on, you must immediately stand up and answer the question in a well-developed impromptu speech. For instance, the moderator might identify the topic "drunk driving" and ask specific questions such as, "Would required driver's education courses help cut down on drunk driving accidents in the United States?" and "Should the penalties for drunk drivers be more strict?" If the class chooses, you may vote at the end of the activity to determine who was the most effective soapbox speaker.

Famous Speech

Copy a famous speech, such as Lincoln's Gettysburg Address or Martin Luther King, Jr.'s "I Have a Dream" speech. Practice and perform the speech using either a manuscript or from memory. This allows you to focus on the delivery of speeches in the manuscript or memorized mode without having to worry about content.

ASSIGNMENTS

An Explanation of the Objectives and Purposes of the Assignments Designed to Support the Material Teaching the Use of Different Modes of Speaking

Impromptu Speech

The impromptu speech is one of the most valuable exercises for beginning speech students as it teaches the importance of thinking quickly, demonstrates the necessity of effective speech organization, and can be a fun and challenging exercise. In addition to the impromptu speaking assignment, sample impromptu topics are included, ranging from the fun and light-hearted to examples that are more serious. Both types of topics have advantages and disadvantages. The topics that are not as serious can be more fun and less intimidating for speakers, but can actually be more difficult to speak on as there sometimes seems to be few serious points to make about them. The more serious topics initially seem difficult, but can actually be easier to discuss as there are more significant issues surrounding them.

OBJECTIVES

1. To allow an opportunity to practice speaking in the impromptu mode.

Oratory

The oratory is perhaps the most commonly assigned type of memorized speech in speech classes. Also, since oratorical-type events are used in both high school and college forensics competition, it is a commonly used speech form. The sample assignment provided here requires the delivery of a speech that is essentially a simplified and condensed version of a competitive oratory. Included with the assignment is a list of the steps necessary in the preparation of an oratory. This is to help speakers focus their efforts in preparation for this assignment.

OBJECTIVES

1. To allow an opportunity to practice speaking in the memorized mode.

2. To teach the proper use of research and outside evidence in speeches.

ASSIGNMENT
Impromptu Speech

Assignment

You will have two minutes to prepare an impromptu speech, which will be delivered to the class immediately at the conclusion of your preparation time. You will draw three topics at random, choose one, and return the other two. You will then deliver a speech that is well organized, makes logical points that are well supported through examples and reasoning, and is between two and three minutes in length.

Due to the lack of preparation time, it is essential that you remember the skills of impromptu speaking and organize your ideas in a logical structure. You will be allowed to use a note card which may be used for notes during the preparation time and for reference during the speech.

Other Requirements

TIME: 2 to 3 minutes

DUE DATE:

IMPROMPTU TOPICS — LIST I

shoes	the telephone	gorillas
feet	parents	high school
balloons	love	hate
movies	ghosts	dentists
ESP	mathematics	history
dancing	vacations	family
grandparents	sisters	brothers
government	shopping malls	baseball
ice cream	birthdays	crime
smoking	candy	babies
Halloween	Thanksgiving	Christmas
steak	men	women
dating	campfires	soccer
popcorn	buttons	shoelaces
mustaches	clowns	gambling
buses	hamburgers	teeth
knives	divorce	the dictionary
happiness	motorcycles	football
college	jobs	monkeys
cheating	prison	the zoo
elementary school	baldness	cleaning
fast food	exercise	meatloaf
Easter	farms	automobiles
Europe	Canada	watches
cows	hot dogs	church
common sense	ice skating	chocolate
tennis	fighting	computers
dishwashers	fingers	horses

IMPROMPTU TOPICS — LIST II

Do teenagers today have more stress than teens in the past?

Considering that drinking and driving kills millions of people each year, should the penalties for DUI be tougher?

Should euthanasia be legalized?

Do Americans watch too much television?

Should prayer be allowed in public schools?

Are too many people today followers, afraid of being individuals?

Do violent TV shows cause children to be more violent?

Is capital punishment cruel, or is it an effective means of controlling crime?

Is prejudice still a problem in America?

Are competitive sports overemphasized in public schools?

Should new cars be required to have air bags for added safety, even though it may drive prices up?

Should gossip magazines, like the *National Enquirer*, be allowed to exist?

What special qualities do good teachers have?

What should the U.S. do to fight drugs?

Should professional athletes be subject to mandatory drug testing or is that a violation of their rights?

Should there be mandatory seat belt laws or is the decision to wear a seat belt an individual choice?

Should doctors with AIDS be allowed to practice?

Should the Army allow women to serve in combat?

Should sex education be taught in schools?

What is your idea of the perfect job?

Is the President of the United States doing a good job? Why or why not?

Oratory

Assignment

Deliver an oratory, which must be scripted and then memorized. The thesis of your speech must be persuasive in nature. That is, you should encourage the audience to take a certain action or adopt a certain belief.

Topic Ideas

You may speak on any topic you choose as long as it has some persuasive point. As always, topics that are creative, original, and make a significant point are the most successful. Some ideas:

Controversial current events

The importance of exercise

The importance of school involvement

Self-esteem

Loneliness

Coping effectively with grief

The benefits of volunteerism

Time management

Why honesty matters

The dangers of stereotyping

The importance of having a positive attitude

Other Requirements

You must use outside evidence (at least three different sources) and directly quote from them or refer to them in your speech.

When research is used, a complete source citation must be provided.

Your speech must be memorized. You will turn in a script to the instructor before you begin speaking and your grade will depend, in part, on how well the speech is memorized.

Because your delivery can be carefully prepared and practiced, you are expected to deliver a strong, persuasive speech.

You may not use a podium or a lectern.

TIME: 3 to 5 minutes

DUE DATE:

STEPS IN THE PREPARATION
OF AN ORATORY

1. Find a topic (brainstorm ideas, get feedback from others, choose one)

2. Research (find as many articles, books, etc., as possible on the subject)

3. Read and examine the research

4. Outline (remember to use an introduction, conclusion, and to break speech down into main ideas)

5. Write first draft of script

6. Revise script and cut to time
   (check organization, development of ideas, use of language, grammar, and length)

7. Plan delivery (decide how speech should sound and how it should be performed)

8. Memorize

9. Practice (remember to use facial expressions, gestures, movement, and vocal techniques)

10. Perform

Speaking With Different Purposes

Delivering Persuasive, Informative,
and Entertaining Speeches

Introduction

When different people speak, they have different objectives in mind. Teachers hope to impart essential knowledge to students. Politicians, lobbyists, and salespeople hope to sway others to a certain way of thinking and to elicit a specific response from their audience. Comedians attempt to entertain those listening to them. Likewise, individuals will not always attempt to accomplish the same purposes each time they speak. An office worker may demonstrate how certain procedures are done to new employees in the morning and deliver a proposal to his or her boss in the afternoon. Certainly, the purposes of these two speeches vary greatly. Sometimes, more than one purpose may be accomplished in the same presentation. A motivational speaker may inform the audience about a technique to help them achieve success, persuade them to use it, and employ humor to maintain their attention.

Because of this, it is important that speakers are trained to speak with different purposes in mind. This chapter focuses on three different types of speaking that can be invaluable to learn: persuasive speaking, informative speaking, and speaking to entertain. Instruction in these types of presentation is essential for two reasons. First, all speakers will, at one time or another, be called upon to use these skills. Second, the methods, styles, and strategies of each type of speaking vary greatly. To be an effective speaker, an individual must know the skills of each type of presentation.

The instruction in this chapter explains the nature of each type of speech situation and gives suggestions to help you effectively deliver each type of speech. No informal classroom activities directly relate to the objectives of the chapter, but activities from other chapters may be applied. For instance, the introductory activities in Chapter One can provide practice in informative speaking and the impromptu and memorized activities in Chapter Five, such as the pet peeve speech and the desperate plea, can provide practice in persuasive speaking. Versatility and adaptability are essential qualities of an effective speaker. This chapter will help you acquire these traits.

PERSUASIVE SPEAKING

Like the tattooist who told his girlfriend, "I have designs on you," persuasive speakers have designs on their audiences. In their book *Persuasive Communication*, Erwin Bettinghaus and Michael Cody state that persuasion is "a conscious attempt by one individual to change the attitudes, beliefs, or behavior of another individual or group through the transmission of some message." In plain English, this means that if you say something to someone that makes them believe something or do something, you have persuaded them. In fact, these two objectives — influencing thinking and motivating action — are the primary goals of persuasive speaking. However, in order to accomplish these two objectives, a speaker must be familiar with the principles and skills of effective persuasive speaking.

An Historical View of Persuasion

Way back in the fourth century B.C., Aristotle identified three major elements that are necessary for an argument to be persuasive. These apply even today.

1. *Logos: the logic of an argument.* First and foremost, an argument has to make sense. It has to be logical, well supported by a number of experts in the field, and within the realm of the audience's experience.

2. *Pathos: the emotion of an argument.* A persuasive message should also appeal to the emotions of the audience. To do this, arguments should be supported with concrete examples to show the audience that the speech can directly relate to them or to people like them.

3. *Ethos: the credibility of the speaker.* In order to build credibility, speakers need to dress properly, act professionally, use believable, well-documented sources, and have charisma. A credible speaker is liked and trusted by the audience.

Suggestions for the Effective Delivery of a Persuasive Speech

Some suggestions can help you be more persuasive when you speak.

1. *Relate the speech to the interests of the listeners.* Many audience members seem to approach a speech with an attitude of "Why should I care? What's in it for me?" It is the job of the persuasive speaker to show the audience that the message is important to them. If your listeners believe they will personally benefit from your speech, they will listen with intense interest.

2. *Build credibility.* As already mentioned, you need to act in a manner that will make the audience believe you and trust you. Show that you have expertise in the subject you are discussing, be honest, and demonstrate that you are similar to the audience in some way.

3. *Use evidence.* Quoting from experts in a field will make your speech much more believable and will also make you seem more credible to the audience as it proves you've "done your homework."

4. *Appeal to both the logic and emotion of the audience.*

INFORMATIVE SPEAKING

Another common speaking situation in which presenters are commonly engaged is the informative speech. The purpose of an informative speech is to teach an audience something, to impart information. Teachers are informative speakers, as are newscasters or anyone who demonstrates a procedure or process. Informative speaking is vitally important. Without it, information could never be passed from one person to another.

Informative speakers generally have three objectives in mind. First, they need to generate enough interest in the information to motivate the audience to listen to them. Second, they must explain the information in such a way that the audience can understand it. Finally, they need to present information in a manner that will enable the audience to retain it after the presentation. Some suggestions follow to help you achieve these goals when you are called upon to deliver an informative speech.

Suggestions for Effective Delivery of an Informative Speech

1. *Don't overestimate or underestimate what your listeners know.* In almost all speaking situations, the audience members have different levels of education, knowledge, and background experiences. Therefore, you must be careful you don't use terminology or discuss concepts that some members of the audience may not know. However, by the same token, you don't want to underestimate your listeners' knowledge and insult them by "talking down" to them. A good rule of thumb: as much as possible, determine the average amount of background information that is held by your audience. However, if you are unsure that all members of your audience are familiar with a term or concept, play it safe and provide an explanation.

2. *Emphasize how your listeners can benefit from your information.* If you increase the reward factor for an audience, you will also increase their attentiveness.

3. *Relate your information to the interests of your audience.* In short, use concepts that are familiar to your audience to explain concepts that aren't. For instance, a high school government teacher could draw an analogy between the federal government and a high school administration. Since students are typically more familiar with their school, this will make it easier for them to understand a concept related to the government.

4. *Try to get the audience to participate.* The more active your audience is, the more likely they are to enjoy the

experience of listening and to remember the facts being presented. Distribute an outline of the presentaion, use a fun quiz on the material being presented, use volunteers to demonstrate a principle, or have the audience directly follow your instructions. Be careful, however, that such tactics do not distract from your presentation.

5. ***Organize your material clearly and logically.*** As with all speeches, an audience is more likely to remember material that is clearly and logically structured.

6. ***Make your information interesting.*** Again, this increases audience interest in the material and retention of the information presented. Use as many techniques as you can, including humor, quotations, visual aids, etc.

SPEAKING TO ENTERTAIN

Speeches to entertain, sometimes called after-dinner speeches because they are often delivered after a meal at a banquet or program, have the primary purpose of entertaining the audience and providing an enjoyable listening experience. Usually, humor is the primary means used to entertain an audience and the strategy that will be discussed here. However, other techniques (such as magic tricks) can also be used. It is also important to note that in most speaking situations, humor is employed not as an end in itself, but to support another purpose. For this reason, speeches to entertain usually have a serious point, and use humor to help make that point.

Even if you don't plan to give a speech to entertain, learning to use humor in speeches can be invaluable. There are many reasons humor should be used in all types of speeches. First, it relaxes the audience and breaks the ice between the speaker and the audience. Also, humor makes the content of any type of speech more interesting and keeps the audience more actively involved. Therefore, knowing how to properly include humor in speeches can be a valuable tool for any speaker.

Suggestions for Effective Use of Humor in a Speech

1. *Use humor that relates to your speech subject.* Humor should always support the points of your speech. Never use a joke just for the sake of the joke. Your audience will wonder what it has to do with them and why you chose to use your speaking time for something irrelevant.

2. *Be creative.* Use humor that is fresh and original. Stay away from old, stale jokes.

3. *Build a humor file.* Have you ever heard a really good joke or expression, but forgotten it before you had a chance to repeat it? Often, speakers are not faced with a lack of jokes available to them when they try to use humor in a speech, but rather, a problem with remembering them. The best way to remedy this is to create a humor file. When you see a cartoon that is especially insightful, read a funny article, or hear a good joke, put it in your file. After time, you will have a tremendous resource to use whenever you prepare a speech.

Suggestions for the Delivery of Humor in a Speech

1. *Never announce humor.* Don't lead into a joke with a phrase like, "I just have to tell you this funny story I heard." This kills the joke, as it makes it seem forced and less spontaneous.

2. *Don't put down your jokes when you tell them.* Leading into a joke with a phrase such as "You may not think this is funny, but . . ." is sure to convince your audience that the joke really *isn't* funny.

3. *Never read anecdotes, humorous stories, or jokes.* This also causes humor to sound artificial and forced.

Even though many speeches are explicitly persuasive, informative, or entertaining, all of these delivery techniques

105

can be used to some degree in all speaking situations. Applying the principles that will allow you to use these techniques effectively can make you a more versatile and competent speaker.

ASSIGNMENTS

An Explanation of the Objectives and Purposes of the Assignments Designed to Support the Material Teaching the Preparation of Speeches With Different Purposes

Persuasive Speech

Ellen M. Anderson and Fred L. Hamel note in the *English Journal* that "Students have difficulty presenting full or convincing arguments because they have little experience with well-reasoned argumentation, not surprising in a society that does much of its persuading in thirty-second sound bites." Through this statement, Anderson and Hamel demonstrate the vital importance of an assignment such as the persuasive speech.

OBJECTIVES

1. To allow an opportunity to practice the skills of persuasive speaking.

2. To teach the concepts of ethos, pathos, and logos and demonstrate their importance in persuasive speech situations.

3. To teach patterns of internal organization in speeches.

Informative Speech

There are innumerable situations in which speakers must provide informative messages. Some occupations, such as teaching, medicine, and broadcasting, require the delivery of such messages on a daily basis. Additionally, the skills of informative speaking can help a speaker in other situations. For instance, a persuasive speaker must educate an audience about a problem before motivating them to help solve that problem.

OBJECTIVES

1. To allow an opportunity to practice the skills of informa-

107

tive speaking.

2. To demonstrate the necessity of clear description and narration in all speaking situations.

After Dinner Speech

As previously noted, humor can be a tremendous tool for speakers. While the after dinner speech may be initially intimidating, it is an effective tool for training speakers to enhance their presentation style by including humor and other techniques that make speeches more enjoyable.

OBJECTIVES

1. To allow an opportunity to practice using humor in speeches.

2. To demonstrate how humor can enhance all types of speeches.

ASSIGNMENT
Persuasive Speech

Assignment

Deliver a speech that is persuasive, or argumentative, in nature. Your job as a speaker is to influence the thinking and actions of the audience. That is, you should sway them to your way of thinking and convince them to take action accordingly. You should use both emotional and logical appeals and establish yourself as a credible speaker. Also, you should use a pattern of organization appropriate for a persuasive speech.

Topic Ideas

There is an almost endless supply of available persuasive topics. Below are some major categories into which many persuasive speeches fall. You might find an idea related to one of these categories.

1. Current events — persuade people to take a stand on a controversial current issue.

2. Motivational — encourage the audience to do something that is good for them, such as staying in school or reading more.

3. Health issues — persuade the audience to participate in activities or consume foods that contribute to good health.

4. Educational issues — show reasons for educational reform, restructuring, or other issues related to education.

Other Requirements

TIME: 3 to 6 minutes

DUE DATE:

Informative Speech

Assignment

Deliver a speech that is designed to teach the audience about a certain subject. As a speaker, you should not take a stand on an issue or attempt to include a persuasive point, but rather, give facts and information to educate the audience about your topic. If you choose, visuals may be used to enhance your presentation. However, they should look professional and be manipulated effectively.

Topic Ideas

1. New technology (cars of the future, the latest airplane technology, new developments in artificial body parts)

2. The paranormal (UFOs, the Loch Ness Monster, Atlantis, Stonehenge)

3. Psychological issues (children's development, schizophrenia, addictions)

4. Hobbies (bowling, mountain climbing, skiing, dance)

5. Music (the biography of a composer, current jazz movements, the history of rock)

6. Sports (the history of a sport, unusual sports)

7. Historical issues

Other Requirements

TIME: 3 to 6 minutes

DUE DATE:

ASSIGNMENT
After Dinner Speech

Assignment

The purpose of an after dinner speech is to make a serious point to the audience, but to use humor and other techniques to make the speech entertaining. The serious point can be any type of a thesis — persuasive, informative, or motivational.

Topic Ideas

Typically, any subject can be comical, though some do lend themselves more readily to humor. You may want to choose such a subject. Below is a list of topics that have been used effectively as after dinner speeches. As you read through it, note how these subjects could be comical and how they could have different types of serious points.

1. How to deal with mistakes and learn from them
2. Educational reform
3. The benefits of acupuncture
4. The strange and quirky nature of the English language
5. What happens when competition is overemphasized
6. The dangers of stereotyping and labeling groups of people
7. The importance of physical fitness
8. The benefits of being a nonconformist
9. How to deal with embarrassing situations

Other Requirements

Humor must be in good taste. A good rule of thumb for what is appropriate: if you are not sure if a joke is acceptable, don't include it!

TIME: 3 to 6 minutes

DUE DATE:

Oral Interpretation
of Literature

The Principles and Skills of Storytelling
and Oral Intrepretation

Introduction

If it is true, as Shakespeare suggests, that all the world is a stage and all men and women performers, then oral interpretation of literature is one of the most natural and essential types of expression. Certainly it is a valuable skill for students in speech courses. For these reasons, it is the focus of this chapter.

There are a number of benefits incurred from the inclusion of oral interpretation of literature in a course of study on speech. First, it is an exercise that requires performers to use their voices and bodies to the fullest extent. Therefore, it helps speakers increase their expressiveness in all speaking and presentation situations. Second, it provides an outlet for individuals who are more interested in performing than speaking. Many people find it easier to present in front of a group if they are playing a character or reading literature than if they are presenting their own speech. Also, because oral interpretation is similar to acting, it can serve as an introduction to acting and theatre. Who knows? You may even want to pursue theatre further after trying oral interpretation.

Also, interpretation requires the analysis of literature and provides an opportunity to practice this skill. Finally, since forensics competitions at both the high school and college levels feature oral interpretation, it is a valuable skill for anyone who may be interested in joining competitive speech to learn.

The instructional section of this chapter defines oral interpretation, illustrates the differences between interpretation and acting, and lists the steps of the process of preparing an oral interpretation, including selecting a piece, writing an introduction, cutting to time, analyzing literature, and performing the piece. The activities and assignments afford opportunities for you to practice the skills of both interpretation and storytelling. A storytelling assignment is included because it is a type of presentation very similar to interpretation and can serve as an effective introduction to or substitute for an interpretation assignment.

ORAL INTERPRETATION OF LITERATURE

Charlotte Lee and Timothy Gura define oral interpretation of literature, or interp, in their book *Oral Interpretation* as "the art of communicating to an audience a work of literary art in its intellectual, emotional, and aesthetic entirety." Simply, this means to read a piece of literature aloud to an audience to show your view, or interpretation, of the meaning of the literature. Carol Marrs says that oral interpretation is "an enlightening way to share the wonderful world of literature with other people." Most importantly, interp is fun — fun to perform, and, if it is done correctly, fun to watch.

The Basics

Oral interpretation is nothing new — it has its roots in ancient times. Before printing was invented, literature was passed on orally. Stories, poems, and songs were used to teach history, customs, laws, and traditions. Obviously, interpretation is no longer a necessary craft. But it is still interesting and can give meaning to literature far more powerful than can a simple reading. Any type of literature may be used in oral interpretation — prose, poetry, or drama.

It is very important to remember that *interpretation is not just reading a story aloud!* It is your job to read the literature in such a way that it shows your interpretation, or view, of the literature and gives the audience a new insight to the story, play, or poem you are reading. It is your job to captivate the audience. Think of it this way: have you ever been so involved in a television program or a movie that you completely blocked out the world around you? That is how your audience should be when they watch you. You cannot capture an audience in this way if you simply read. You must use your voice, body, and other techniques to make your performance powerful and captivating.

117

Finding a Piece of Literature

Finding the piece of literature you will perform is perhaps the most important and difficult part of preparing an interp. This is often made more difficult by the fact that we, as Americans, don't read as much as we should. Therefore, when we think of what we can perform, our choices are often narrow and duplicate the choices made by other interpers.

Still, it is absolutely essential to your success as an interper that you find a piece that fits you, has dramatic or humorous impact, and is fresh, original, and relevant. There are a number of factors to consider when choosing a piece to perform.

Factors in Choosing an Interp Piece

1. *Find a piece of literature that fits you and which you enjoy.* First, the piece must be interesting to you. Otherwise, you will become bored with it and it will consequently bore the audience. Also, it must be a piece that fits and showcases your talents — it should not be too easy nor too difficult for you.

2. *Consider your audience.* The piece should also be interesting and relevant to your audience. After all, they are the ones you are trying to entertain. Because of this, it is important to choose a piece with *universal appeal*, one that deals with themes that are common to all of mankind and of interest to all types of audiences.

3. *Choose literature that is of literary merit, or of high quality.* This means that the piece of literature you select must be appropriate and effectively manipulate literary techniques such as theme, metaphor, symbolism, etc. Literary merit is not absolute and is up for debate. However, there are certain factors you should look for when you consider if a piece is good literature.

Factors That Determine Literary Merit

1. *Universality.* This means that the main idea or the theme of a work is potentially interesting to all people because it touches upon a common experience. It deals with emotions that all of us have felt. For instance, Shakespeare's works are still incredibly popular today, centuries after he wrote them, because they deal with universal themes such as love, hate, jealousy, fear and despair.

2. *Individuality.* This refers to the writer's fresh, unique approach to a universal subject. This can be created through the use of language, imagery, organization, etc. If you've ever watched situation comedies on television you've seen examples of work that is *not* individual in nature, as they almost all follow the same format and use the same ideas.

3. *Suggestion.* This means that literature of merit leaves the audience with something to do. Everything is not stated on an immediate level, but the readers must interpret and analyze the literature according to their own experiences. Because of suggestion, different readers can gain different lessons from the same piece of literature.

Though all of these qualities may not be equal in a piece of literature, you don't want to select a piece of literature to perform if it is missing or weak in any of these three factors.

Introductions

In oral interpretation, an introduction to the performance is required. The introduction has three very important purposes.

1. To get the attention of the audience.

2. To introduce the title, author, and significance of the literature.

3. To set the scene being performed and to give background information regarding it.

Hints for Writing Effective Introductions

1. ***Get the attention of the audience.*** Use the introduction to grab the audience and make them want to listen to your piece. There are many ways to do this.

   — Use a teaser. This is a dramatic piece of the literature that will be especially interesting to the audience. For instance, say you're watching your favorite show on television and during the commercial they show a fifteen-second clip from the show that comes next. This is a teaser as it is designed to catch your attention and "tease" you by not revealing how the scene will end so that you'll want to watch the next show as well.

   — Relate the work to the lives of your audience. Find how the literature you're performing is relevant to your audience and emphasize that.

   — Use a quotation from a well-known individual.

   — Begin with a rhetorical question.

   — Relate the literature to a current event.

   — Find your own technique. The important thing is that you grab your audience at the very beginning.

2. ***Set up the piece of literature.*** First, you need to briefly introduce the plot, theme, and characters that will be important in your performance. Create the mood and establish the setting. Also, if you are performing a scene from a larger work, tell what happened before your selection. Pretend your friend entered a movie fifteen minutes late and you are telling him what he missed. Also, briefly preview the events that occur in your selection. Just make sure that the audience will be able to follow your performance. No one will pay attention to something they don't understand.

3. *Give the name of the title and author.* We need to know what we're listening to, so absolutely do not forget this!

Cutting

This refers to cutting a piece of literature so that it can be performed, along with an introduction, in a certain period of time. It is important to know that practically all pieces of literature can be cut so that they can be effectively performed within a certain time frame.

Tips for Cutting Literature to Time

1. *Try to find shorter pieces.* The shorter the work, the less you have to cut. Very short stories or poems are useful because you can keep almost all of the work, which makes it easier for the audience to understand and maintains the literary integrity of the piece.

2. *If using a longer work, try to find a specific scene or episode that, by itself, fills the time limit.* It's better to avoid skipping all over a story. Again, this will confuse your audience.

3. *Always cut "he said," "she said," and adjectives that can be* shown *through your performance.* Since you are performing, you can adopt a different voice and physical manner to show who is speaking and how they are speaking. The only exceptions are in poetry when all words are needed to maintain the rhythm of the poem and when one character is quoting another.

4. *Have a purpose for your performance and cut things that do not help you accomplish that purpose.* Think what you want to show about a piece of literature and choose narration and dialog that contributes to your purpose. For instance, if you want to emphasize a certain theme in a novel, choose scenes in which that theme is emphasized or illustrated and perform only those scenes.

Analysis

Many interpers become so focused on their performance that they forget the title of the craft they are practicing: oral *interpretation* of literature. Before you can perform your interpretation of a piece of literature or bring a new insight to the piece you are performing, you must analyze the literature to determine your interpretation of its meaning, characterization, mood, etc. First, there are some terms you need to know to be able to do so.

Literary Techniques and Attributes

1. ***Climax.*** The climax of a piece of literature is the point of highest action and emotional impact in the plot. It is sometimes called the turning point of the story. It is at this point the level of drama and intensity in a performance should be highest.

2. ***Characterization.*** Each character in a work is given a unique personality by the author. Also, all characters have different motives that determine their actions. You need to understand these before you can bring the characters to life.

3. ***Imagery.*** This refers to the images and mood created by the author through a variety of techniques. As the performer, it is your job to allow the audience to see the same images you see as you perform the piece and to create a certain mood to characterize your interpretation.

4. ***Variety and Contrast.*** Variety is provided when two things of the same type differ in certain details. For instance, two characters might have the same age, sex, and background, but choose to express themselves differently. Contrast is more of a sharp distinction. It refers to opposition or differences between things. For instance, two characters might be completely different from each other, which is bound to affect their interaction. It is your job as an interper to determine if the author of your piece

has used either variety or contrast and to reveal this in your performance or characterization of the individuals involved.

5. ***Balance.*** This refers to the proportion of content on either side of the climax. As a performer, you need to understand this so you don't overemphasize or underemphasize certain sections of a work. For example, some dramatic interpers will maintain a very high intensity throughout a piece, with no variance in emotional level. This not only tires the performer and the audience, it also prevents the interper from emphasizing the parts that are truly dramatic.

6. ***Rhythm.*** The way the words sound and language flows is the rhythm of the piece. You need to follow this rhythm to provide a smooth, fluent delivery. This is especially true in interpretation of poetry. However, be careful you don't take this too far: often, poetic interpers will fall into a sing-song pattern of speech, which can be very annoying.

As you've probably guessed, analysis of a piece of literature is not easy. For this reason, many interpers skip it. Don't do this! It can mean the difference between a great interpretation and one that is mediocre.

Steps in Analysis of Literature

1. ***Read the entire work.*** Even if you are performing a short scene from a novel or a long play, you need to read the entire work to understand it as a whole and to determine how your selection fits in with the literature in its entirety.

2. ***Determine your impressions and feelings.*** Ask, after reading the literature, how it makes you feel and what it makes you think. Perhaps you can even write down your initial impressions so that you can recreate those feelings when you perform.

3. ***Analyze the literary techniques in your selection.*** Go

through the piece and determine how the literary techniques used by the author interact and affect the literature.

Marking the Manuscript

Let's review — you've chosen a piece to perform, analyzed it, written an introduction, and cut it to time. You're ready to work on the performance, right? Almost, but there's still one more thing you must do first to help you prepare. This is to mark the script to assure the best possible reading. Some suggestions to help you do so:

1. *Make a number of photocopies of the script.* This allows you to make a mess of a couple while determining how to perform the piece and still have clean copies to re-mark neatly to use for performance.

2. *Cut sections not to be performed neatly and completely.* Make sure there is no doubt what you are *not* reading.

3. *Underline words and phrases to emphasize.* This will help you remember the key parts that deserve special emphasis and attention.

4. *Highlight in different colors the dialog of different characters.* Many performers find this helpful in keeping the different characters clear and distinct.

5. *Write notes to yourself in the margin.* Write anything you want to remember to include in your performance in the margin of the script. If you see it there long enough, it will become second nature when you perform.

Delivery

Now you're finally ready to work on the actual performance of the interpretation. However, it is important to remember that no performer can do an adequate job performing literature with no thought or preparation. Rather, an effective performance requires a great deal of planning. As you plan your performance, there are two aspects of delivery on which you need to focus: the vocal performance and the physical performance. According to Charlotte Lee and Timothy Gura, authors of *Oral Interpretation*, "Body and voice together become a twofold instrument, and the modern interpreter must learn to control and coordinate them perfectly in order to communicate the full meaning of the literature." The way you use these two aspects of delivery determines the dramatic, humorous, or emotional impact your piece will have upon the listener. You absolutely cannot ignore either aspect and still present an adequate performance. We'll consider them one at a time.

The Vocal Aspect of Delivery in Interpretation

This includes everything you can do with your voice to add to your performance. You need to be sure, first and foremost, that we can hear and understand you. To do so, be sure you project your voice to the back of the room, speak clearly, and articulate and enunciate all words. Also, by using inflection and vocal variance, you can give emphasis to certain sections of your work and keep the performance interesting. Finally, you can use vocal techniques such as rate, inflection, tone, volume, etc., to create emotion and meaning in a performance. A few additional suggestions can help you use your voice to make your performance really powerful.

1. ***Don't over-perform.*** Many competitors believe that the louder or the shakier or the more different their voice sounds, the more dramatic they are. Wrong!

2. ***Try to sound as natural as possible.*** Think how the character you are performing would sound, and try to sound like that character — not an exaggeration of that character.

3. **Make different voices for different characters sound different, but authentic.** If the voices of two characters are too similar, the audience will be confused as to who is speaking.

4. **Don't attempt any accent you can't handle.** Be very critical of any accent or imitation you want to use and discard it if it is not effective or accurate.

5. **If you can do an accent, do it!** Assuming, of course, it fits the piece you are performing. One thing, though: if you do use an accent, be consistent with it throughout the entire performance. It is better to not even attempt an accent than to slip in and out of it.

6. **Give your voice variance.** As with any performance, you want to avoid a monotone delivery.

7. **Use your voice to emphasize climaxes.** Remember, in order to do this, you need to tone down the other parts so that the audience will be able to distinguish between what's important and what's more important. If you are as intense as you can be throughout the entire piece, you will lose your dramatic edge.

The Physical Aspect of Delivery in Interpretation

While it is sometimes easy for interpers, especially beginners, to forget to use their bodies to enhance their performances, it is just as important to plan and use the physical aspects of delivery as the vocal aspects to show emotion, characterization, and to give power to the performance. There are a number of ways the body can be used to enhance performance.

1. **Gestures.** The most obvious area in which the body can be used is through the gestures made to emphasize points. Remember, anything you do in front of a group might seem very large and feel silly, but will appear small and

hardly noticeable to the audience. Therefore, it is imperative that you make your gestures and movements *big*. Also, if you use too many gestures, they will become distracting, but if you use too few, they won't enhance your performance.

2. *Facial expressions.* Sometime, while you are watching a television program, notice what proportion of the shots are close-ups of the actors. The majority of the time, while we are watching television, we see only the faces of the actors, not their entire bodies. Therefore, the way they use their faces is very important. Watch how they do so — how their expressions, responses, etc., reveal thought and emotion. You can also do the same while you are interping.

3. *Posture and muscle tone.* Posture can show age, health, and general state of mind. A person who is young, healthy, and in a state of controlled relaxation will exhibit tall, strong posture. Older, sick, and less confident people may exhibit posture that is not as strong. Also, muscle tone, or the general amount of relaxation in the body, can also reveal much about an individual's character or state of mind. A good interper will use these characteristics to show the emotional and physical state of the characters they are performing.

Again, don't forget to use your body, as well as your voice, to add drama and meaning to your performance. There are a few more things you should remember. First, as with vocal aspects, don't overact. Try for gestures and facial expressions that are expressive, but natural. Also, an interesting phenomenon that occurs in oral interpretation performances is that the audience will mimic the responses of the performer. This is especially true if the performer is a talented, experienced interper. If the performer is relaxed and loose, the audience will be relaxed and loose. If the performer is tense, the audience will also be tense. Therefore, you can use your body to emphasize the mood of the cutting and to show climaxes. Bring your audience in more fully at the climaxes of your cutting by demonstrating a more tense posture and gesturing. Let them relax in between by being more relaxed. Use your body to keep the audience on the edge of their seats!

Performing Multiple Characters

One of the characteristics of interpretation of literature is that a performer will often assume the role of more than one character. When students new to interp learn this, they ask, "How do you do that?" and "Doesn't that look silly?" Actually, it is not that difficult to do if you know how, and, if it is done correctly, it will not look silly at all.

1. **Use focus points.** Focus points are imaginary points somewhere at the back of the audience to which performers point their stance and gaze when they are performing specific characters. *If you are performing a cutting that requires you to play the part of two or more characters, it is absolutely essential that you use focus points!*

   There are two purposes for the use of focus points in an interpretation of literature. First, it helps the audience keep the characters separated. Second, it gives the interper a point of focus in the audience to imagine where the scene is occurring. Typically, focus points should be no more than thirty degrees apart. This means that you should turn your body no more than fifteen degrees off center for each character. Otherwise, you end up swaying, which can distract from your performance.

2. **Use different voices for different characters.** Be sure that the voices used for different characters are not too similar or the audience will become confused. Remember, though, all voices used should sound natural and authentic.

3. **Create a different physical manner for each character.** Allow different characters to exhibit different postures,

gestures, expressions, and levels of relaxation. In this way, you can distinguish the characters physically as well as vocally.

4. **Be consistent in all you do.** Throughout your performance, be sure that your focus points, vocal techniques, and physical techniques used for each character are consistent. If you change any or slip out of any of these techniques, the audience will become confused and will lose track of your performance.

Differences Between Interpretation and Acting

One of the more confusing concepts for new interpers to grasp is the fact that, although interpretation of literature and acting are very similar, they are not the same. There are four fundamental differences between acting and interpretation of which you need to be aware so you don't cross over the line and begin to act in an interp.

1. **No props are used in interp.** A performer will use his body to suggest the presence of an object, but cannot use the actual object in the performance.

2. **A manuscript is used in interp.** Ostensibly, you are allowed to read an interp cutting. Of course, performers who completely read their pieces are not left as free to use the vocal and physical aspects of delivery to enhance the performance. Therefore, for an effective performance, a script should be eighty to ninety percent memorized by the interper. The reason scripts are required is that they remind the audience that the performer is interpreting someone else's work and not actually assuming the part of a character as an actor would.

3. **You are not allowed to move in interp.** Of course, you can gesture and use other physical aspects of delivery, but you are not allowed to walk from one spot to another.

129

4. Interpers often perform the part of more than one character. In acting, this is very rare.

The Actual Performance

You're ready! You've taken all the necessary steps and you are now ready to perform your interpretation for an audience! As you do, there are some things you need to remember.

1. Maintain a professional manner. Your manner should be the same as it would for any presentation in front of a group. Display confidence, enjoy the experience of performing, and try to build a relationship, or rapport, with your audience.

2. Handle your script professionally.

— Put your script in a small binder (about half the size of one you would use to hold notebook paper) or use "backing sheets," which have a solid black backing and a transparent cover.

— Make sure the script you use is clean and neat so it is easy for you to follow. Many interpers will even retype their script to make it more readable.

— Pages should be arranged so you won't turn pages in the middle of a paragraph or verse of poetry. You want the audience to focus on you and your performance, not the way you handle the manuscript.

Final Words

If you have followed all these steps in preparation for your performance, you have no reason to worry as you should do very well. Remember as you perform to always have fun. If interpretation isn't enjoyable for you, the audience will pick up on that and will respond accordingly. Also, in interpretation it is important to let yourself go and to take risks. You will only find the techniques that work through experimentation and the willingness to take chances. Jack Holland and Virgil Sessions of Orange Coast College say, "You may find it hard to express yourself, to show honest emotions. . . . To overcome a habit of repressing emotions is not an easy task, but it must be done if you are to bring out the richness in literature and the richness in yourself . . . so let yourself go!"

CLASSROOM ACTIVITIES

Individual and Group Activities to Provide Opportunities for Practice in the Skills of Storytelling and Oral Interpretation of Literature

OBJECTIVES

Speakers will gain experience and practice in the skills of storytelling and oral interpretation of literature and will learn to be more expressive both physically and vocally.

Anecdote Exchange

Break into small groups of four to six people. In your group, tell an interesting story or anecdote about your life, using as much animation and demonstrating as much enthusiasm as possible. Since you are speaking in front of only a few individuals, this assignment is typically non-threatening and therefore allows you an opportunity to be more expressive than you would in front of a large group.

Most Embarrassing Moment Speech

In small groups or in front of the class, relay the events of a particularly embarrassing moment you suffered. This activity provides a fun and entertaining way to learn narrative techniques and to use humor in a storytelling situation. It also has an added advantage as you get to learn about the most embarrassing moments suffered by your classmates!

Children's Story

Choose your favorite children's story and read it to the class, creating lively characters and using vocal and physical techniques to bring the story to life. Since children's stories are written to be read out loud and are usually silly in nature, you should find them easy to perform in an expressive way.

Original Children's Story

Write your own children's story and perform it for the class. A fun application of this assignment is to take the stories to a daycare center or an elementary school and perform them for children, who are always an appreciative audience. This activity provides the same benefits as reading published stories, but allows you to be more creative.

Charades

A game of charades is not only fun, it can also help develop the physical aspects of performance. The class should be divided into two teams. Each team must first write charade topics for the opposing team in preselected categories (titles of songs, books, movies and television shows work well, as do concrete nouns and action verbs.) After each team submits a sufficient number of topics, the game begins as a member of the first team draws a topic from those submitted by the second team and acts it out for his or her team without speaking. If the team guesses the topic in a given time limit (such as one or two minutes), they receive a point. The second team then takes a turn. The game continues until everyone has had a chance to perform or until a certain amount of time has expired, with the group earning the most points the winner.

Reverse Charades

Traditionally, charades is played when participants act out a topic without speaking, conveying meaning exclusively through physical movements. However, if this traditional pattern is reversed, it demonstrates how the voice can be used to convey emotion. Again, the class is divided into two groups. One member from each group is given a phrase to recite that carries no special significance (such as "the quick brown fox jumped over the lazy dog") and an emotion to demonstrate exclusively through vocal techniques. Gestures, facial expressions, or any other uses of the body are not permitted. The team that guesses the correct emotion first receives a point and then two other participants repeat the process.

Lip Synchronization

Another fun activity that helps develop physical expressiveness is the lip sync. Choose your favorite song and then perform it for the class, moving your lips to the music. You will need to exaggerate lip and body movement and really "ham it up." If you wish, you may use a dead microphone, costumes, and props.

Nonsense Syllable Dialog

Find a partner with whom you can work. You and your partner will be given a certain situation to act out in front of the class (such as a father and son arguing about the son coming home after curfew). You must then perform the scene, speaking only in nonsense syllables like ooga, bunga, ula, and zonga. The class can try to guess what scene is being performed. This activity is beneficial because it requires the use of not only physical but vocal techniques to convey meaning.

Group Poetry Performance

An activity suggested by Allan Wolf in his book *Something Is Going to Happen* is the group performance of poetry. You will work in a performance team and must choose a poem to perform that is especially physical or expressive. Using the poems as scripts, plan, direct, block, and perform the poetry for the class. Wolf asserts that this activity encourages careful reading of poetry and increases appreciation and understanding of poetry. It also provides an opportunity to practice the skills of acting and oral interpretation.

ASSIGNMENTS

An Explanation of the Objectives and Purposes of the Assignments Designed to Support the Material Teaching Effective Performance of an Oral Interpretation of Literature

Storytelling Speech

The storytelling speech is a valuable exercise because it requires the same skills as oral interpretation of literature, but in a less threatening manner. It will give you a good idea of the basics of oral interpretation. In addition, it will allow you to be more expressive without having to engage in a detailed study of storytelling and oral interpretation. You will gain experience in writing fiction, creating characters, and making up exciting situations.

OBJECTIVES

1. To introduce the skills and principles of oral interpretation of literature.

2. To elicit expressiveness in speech delivery.

3. To allow for the employment and development of creativity through the writing of an original story.

Oral Interpretation of Literature

As mentioned in the introduction to this chapter, there are numerous educational benefits to the inclusion of an oral interpretation of literature assignment in the beginning speech class. First, it can be a fun presentation to perform. Many students identify this assignment as their favorite at the end of the term, even if they were not initially excited about the idea of performing literature. Also, it helps speakers improve in all speaking situations as it demonstrates the importance of being expressive and bringing emotion to presentations.

135

OBJECTIVES

1. To allow an opportunity to practice displaying emotion in performance.

2. To provide an introduction to the skills of literature analysis as well as an opportunity to practice those skills.

ASSIGNMENT
Storytelling

Assignment

Write and deliver an original story or narrative. It should be fictional, but can be based on fact if you desire. You may use either real or fictional characters.

As you write your narrative, try to invent a story that will not only captivate the audience, but will also be interesting when read. The use of dialog, unusual characters, and exciting action can help.

As you perform the story, it will be your job to use your voice and body to add interest to the performance. Vocally, you should articulate clearly, use appropriate volume, expression and variety, and use different voices for different characters. Physically, you should use gestures, facial expressions, and other techniques to contribute to the piece and to emphasize emotion and feeling.

Other Requirements

You will speak from a script. However, you should be familiar with the script so you are free to make eye contact and to be expressive in your delivery.

At the conclusion of your presentation, you will turn in the script.

TIME: 3 to 6 minutes

DUE DATE:

Oral Interpretation of Literature

Assignment

Perform an oral interpretation of literature using both physical and vocal techniques to demonstrate your analysis of the literature and to show the emotion in the piece. The literature may be prose, poetry, or drama and must be from a published source. You must adhere to the rules of interpretation. That is, you may not act.

Additionally, you must present an introduction to your selection that accomplishes the three purposes of this type of introduction. The introduction is included in the overall performance time.

Other Requirements

You may use a script in your performance, but should know the piece well enough to effectively perform, rather than being too tied to the script.

The script should look professional and should not distract from the performance in any way.

TIME: 4 to 7 minutes

DUE DATE:

Applied Activities

Using Public Speaking Techniques in
Applied, Real-World Situations

Introduction

In the preface of this book, it was noted that public speaking is one of the most applicable skills you will learn in school as virtually every occupation requires some amount of speaking. This chapter provides activities that require the demonstration of public speaking skills in realistic activities similar to those people engage in every day. These activities include a marketing presentation, talk show, legal debate, and parliamentary debate.

Participation in these activities has numerous advantages and benefits. First, such activities demonstrate the importance of speech in daily life. Second, they allow for practice of skills that are applicable and important in real-world situations. Also, these activities require a higher degree of interaction and involvement by students than most speech assignments and therefore provide a greater opportunity for learning. Finally, they require the use of many skills learned in a public speaking course. For instance, the parliamentary debate requires research, critical listening, reasoning, and the delivery of both prepared and impromptu speeches.

You will notice that no instructional notes or informal activities are included in this chapter. That is because the assignments require the use of skills that you have already learned and practiced. However, the assignments are explained in detail so that you should have little trouble understanding what is required.

Chances are, you will use the skills learned in your public speaking course many times. These activities allow you to combine many of the techniques you have already learned and to see how these skills will be used even when you have completed your speech class.

ASSIGNMENTS

An Explanation of the Objectives and Purposes of the Applied Public Speaking Assignments

Talk Show and Marketing Presentation

These assignments are similar as they both require group participation and the consideration of specific issues. Also, both assignments require speakers to use numerous public speaking skills and techniques in order to be successful.

OBJECTIVES

1. To promote cooperation among group members and to demonstrate how speakers must often collaborate in order to be successful.

2. To allow practice in various public speaking skills, including prepared and impromptu speaking, research, critical thinking and questioning, audience involvement, and the use of visual aids.

3. To encourage audience participation and critical listening through audience involvement.

Legal Debate

Through television and the publicity that surrounds many trials, most everyone is familiar with the basic form of a legal trial, which this assignment uses. However, by participating in a mock legal trial, speakers can greatly benefit as it requires the delivery of various types of speeches, critical thinking, and careful preparation.

What types of cases should be debated? You may use various sources for a trial. Current trials that are commonly known can be debated, or a fictitious crime or civil suit may be created for debate. However, you should try to find a case that is controversial and doesn't seem to provide an inherent advantage for one side so that both sides will have an equal chance to win the debate.

OBJECTIVES

1. To provide practice in different modes of speaking, including manuscript and impromptu speaking.

2. To encourage critical thinking as participants refute and debate the arguments of their opponents.

3. To allow practice in acting and performing skills for the individuals who assume the roles of witnesses.

Parliamentary Debate

This type of debate is very important as it is used by a wide variety of groups and is central to American government and the democratic system. Though parliamentary procedure is briefly explained in the assignment, a more in-depth study of procedure before beginning a parliamentary debate might prove beneficial.

OBJECTIVES

1. To increase familiarity with parliamentary procedure and the nature of parliamentary debate.

2. To allow for practice in various modes of speaking as well as the skills of argumentation.

3. To promote critical thinking and reasoning.

Talk Show

Assignment

As a group, you will prepare and present a fictional television talk show. In the talk show format, you will debate and discuss an issue that is important, relevant, controversial, and timely. Your purpose is to clearly present your subject to the audience so that they will understand both sides of the issue and leave well-informed about the issue. Group members will assume the following roles:

1 Member: Host, or moderator, of the show
2 Members: Experts on the issue being discussed
1-4 Members: Witnesses, or people personally involved
              with the issue

Topic Ideas

You may speak on any topic you choose as long as it meets the criteria listed above. Try to find topics that will interest your audience. As in real talk shows, audience involvement can greatly add interest. Some possible topics are listed.

1. Underage drinking. Is it a major problem? Is alcoholism common in this age group? What can be done to solve the problem?

2. The state of education in America. Are American schools falling behind the rest of the world? How can American schools best be reformed?

3. High school dropouts. Do dropouts create a significant problem? What can be done to reduce the dropout rate?

4. Volunteerism. Do Americans do enough volunteer work? What can be done to encourage people to volunteer more often? Should schools have a community service requirement?

5. The war on drugs. Is America winning the war on drugs? What can be done to better fight drugs?

Other Ideas

To make your presentation more interesting, you may want to use the following ideas:

1. Use visual aids. If properly made, visuals can help clarify issues for your audience and provide additional visual interest to the presentation.

2. Encourage audience involvement. Generating a discussion on the subject or entertaining questions from audience members can help keep them interested and will help clarify issues.

3. Try to make the presentation as authentic as possible. The use of theme music, out-of-the-studio calls, a realistic set, and a creative name for your show can help make your presentation seem like a real talk show. You may even break for a commercial which can provide humor within the presentation.

Other Requirements

You must research your subject and present factual information during the performance. This may best be accomplished either through the host or the "expert" guests.

When research is used, a complete source citation must be provided.

Limited notes may be used, but all group members should know the material well enough to maintain the authentic talk show feel.

TIME: One show should take at least thirty minutes.

DUE DATE:

Marketing Presentation

Assignment

You will work in groups and assume that each group is a marketing team with the job of developing and presenting a marketing strategy for a product or service. You will also assume that your audience is the board of directors whose approval you must gain in order to implement your strategy and to market your product or service. To meet the requirements of the assignment, you must achieve the following objectives:

OBJECTIVES

Presentation: Your group must prepare and perform a ten- to fifteen-minute presentation in which you introduce the members of the group to the board of directors, describe the product or service you will be marketing, the strategy you will use to sell your idea, and the benefits of this product or service to both the public as well as your supporting corporation. During this presentation, each member of the group must take an equal, active role.

Visual Aids: You must prepare two visual aids:

1. The first visual will display the name and logo of your agency.

2. The second visual will be used in your presentation and will demonstrate either how your idea works or its benefits.

Supporting Materials: Create a one-page handout that summarizes and demonstrates (through visuals or detailed description) the message of your presentation.

What Should You Sell?

It is the responsibility of your group to determine what product or service will be marketed. Ideas may range from the common (a lawnmowing service) to the original (an underwater resort). However, you want to gain approval to market your idea from the board of directors. Therefore, you need to be sure that there is a market for your product or service and that you are significantly different from products and services already being sold. In your presentation, you will need to be able to demonstrate that you will meet a consumer need that is not currently being met.

DUE DATE:

ASSIGNMENT
Legal Debate

Assignment

You will participate in a legal debate or mock trial. Different people will assume different roles and responsibilities. It is your job to play the part assigned to you and complete the requirements of your role. Responsibilities will be broken down as follows:

> 3 Prosecuting Attorneys
> 3 Defense Attorneys
> Witnesses (number will vary depending on case)
> Jury Members

Procedure

The debate will proceed as follows:

Opening Statements: Prosecution (four- to six-minute speech)
Opening Statements: Defense (four- to six-minute speech)

Questioning of Witnesses (no time limit)
(Prosecution will call witnesses followed by the defense)

Closing Statements: Defense (four- to six-minute speech)
Closing Statements: Prosecution (four- to six-minute speech)

Jury Conference

Verdict Announced

Responsibilities

ATTORNEYS

Both the prosecution and defense will consist of teams of three lawyers. Their responsibilities will be broken down as follows:

Lawyer 1:   Opening statements
Lawyer 2:   Examination of witnesses
Lawyer 3:   Closing statements

Lawyer 1

Deliver a four- to six-minute speech introducing the case to the jury, stating the issues that will become important in the trial and stating the facts that your side will prove that you believe will win the decision for your side. After your speech, the jury should know the facts of the case, what your arguments will be, and the legal basis for your approach to the trial.

Lawyer 2

Question the witnesses to reveal the facts important in the trial. Before the debate, it is your responsibility to prepare friendly witnesses by telling them what type of questions they will encounter from both you as well as the opposing legal team and to feel out unfriendly witnesses by interviewing them before the debate. Remember — good lawyers never ask a question to which they don't already know the answer. You will need good analytic and reasoning skills to force witnesses to admit facts they may not want to admit. It might be helpful to prepare lines of questions ahead of time, but you also want to remain flexible enough to vary from your list of questions if the situation demands.

Questioning in a legal trial takes the following form: the prosecution calls witnesses to further their case. After witnesses are questioned by the prosecution, they may be cross-examined by the defense. When the prosecution has rested, the defense may call witnesses in rebuttal of the prosecution. These witnesses may be cross-examined by the prosecution if the attorneys so choose.

Lawyer 3

Deliver a four- to six-minute closing speech that summarizes the trial, points out the major issues, explains the significance of statements made during the trial, and gives the jury the legal justifications to vote for your side. It is your job to bring the trial into focus for the jury and to persuade them to vote for your side. Though you will be able to prepare parts of this speech before the trial, much of this speech will need to be prepared as the trial progresses so that you may address the significant events of the trial.

WITNESSES

You will assume the part of one of the people involved in the crime or dispute being debated. It is your job to answer the questions asked of you in a manner that is truthful (in accordance with the known facts of the case) and also beneficial to your side. For instance, if you are a defendant in a criminal trial, you will want to present your testimony so that it will build sympathy and support for your cause among the jury.

JURY

As a member of the jury, it is your responsibility to listen to all the arguments and testimony presented in the trial carefully and to make a decision. It is essential that you base your decision solely on the trial and not on any preconceptions or prejudices you may bring to the trial and that you listen to all testimony with an unbiased ear.

Parliamentary Debate

Assignment

You will participate in a parliamentary debate. A parliamentary debate is one in which a group makes decisions on policy through parliamentary procedure, which is a system of rules and customs designed to provide order to group meetings and to allow groups to make decisions. Most commonly used by law-making groups, such as Congress, parliamentary procedure is also used by a variety of groups including churches, businesses, and service groups. Parliamentary procedure follows three main principles: the will of the majority determines action and policy, the right of the minority to speak and participate must always be protected, and the rules must be followed as they exist to serve the organization and are equally applicable to all members.

Procedure

Each meeting will proceed as follows:

1. Call to order
   (Announces meeting open; made by presiding officer)

2. Reading of minutes of previous meeting
   (Summary of last meeting; done by secretary)

3. Consideration of old business
   (Completion of work begun but not finished at last meeting)

4. Consideration of new business
   (Resolutions will be presented, discussed, and voted on)

5. Call to adjourn
   (Requires a second; needs majority vote to pass)

6. Adjournment
   (Dismissal; made by presiding officer)

Requirements

RESOLUTION:

Definition

A resolution is a generalized statement expressing a belief. The group will consider numerous resolutions and vote on each resolution to determine whether it will pass or fail. If a resolution is passed, it does not carry the force of law. Rather, it is used to express a belief of the group.

A resolution must accomplish two purposes: to outline the reasons some sort of change in the status quo, or current system, should be made (expressed in a "Whereas" statement) and to state the specific action that should be taken (expressed in a "Be it Resolved" statement). Simply, resolutions drive debate. They state the issues that will be debated in a meeting and the action that group members hope the group will take.

Procedure

Before the parliamentary debate begins, an agenda, or schedule, will be set. Each resolution and motion will be considered in its turn. The presiding officer will announce that consideration of a resolution has begun, read the resolution aloud, and then ask the author of the resolution to deliver an authorship speech, which states the reasons the resolution was written and why it should be passed. After the authorship speech is completed, the speaker may open him or herself to the group for questions. The presiding officer may want to set a limit on the number of questions asked to prevent this from consuming too much time. This time must be used exclusively for questioning, not for debate. Two types of questions may be asked: those to clarify issues that may still be cloudy and those that are designed to expose a weakness in the speaker's reasoning.

After the authorship speech is completed, the presiding

officer will open the floor to debate on the resolution. The presiding officer will begin debate by asking for a speech in support of the resolution and then alternate between supporting and opposing speeches. When debate is exhausted, a member of the group may call for a vote by asking for "previous question." In order to pass, previous question must be seconded and receive a majority vote. If previous question fails, debate on the issue will resume. If previous question passes, a vote on the resolution will be taken. Again, a majority vote is required for a resolution to pass.

Amendments to a resolution may be made in four ways: by adding to a resolution, deleting from a resolution, changing text, or dividing a resolution so that two separate issues may be voted on individually. To be considered, an amendment must be proposed, seconded, and deemed by the presiding officer to not change the intent of the resolution. If this occurs, an amendment is considered just as any other motion. It must be discussed, previous question must be called and passed, and a vote must be taken on the amendment. If the amendment does not gain a majority vote, discussion of the original resolution will continue. If the amendment does pass, debate of the amended resolution will begin.

Assignment

Write a resolution on any issue (school, city, nation) that can be debated in the parliamentary debate in class. Your resolution must deal with an issue that can be changed through legislation (you may not impose world peace as there is no way to legislate such a thing, but you may create a cultural exchange to help encourage world peace), and must be controversial. Your resolution must meet the criteria stated above, be clear and concise, and demonstrate proper use of language and grammar. An example is provided following the description of the assignment that you may use as a model.

153

AUTHORSHIP SPEECH:

Definition

An authorship speech is made by the author, or creator, of a resolution and is the first speech given in debate on the resolution. It does not merely restate the resolution, but rather explains, develops, and supports the reasons set forth in the resolution. The author should explain why he or she wrote the resolution as well as the reasons it should be passed.

Assignment

Deliver a three- to seven-minute authorship speech on your resolution. The speech should exhibit all qualities of proper speech making, including organization, use of delivery techniques and research, if applicable. After the speech, open yourself to questions from the floor. To be persuasive, you need to study your issue and prepare yourself for possible questions so that your responses will be accurate and convincing.

SUPPORTING AND OPPOSING SPEECHES:

Definition

These are speeches made by group members either supporting the resolution by expanding on the points made in the authorship speech, bringing up new arguments, and refuting points made in opposing speeches. Or these could be speeches made by group members opposing the resolution by refuting points made by proponents of the resolution and noting reasons to vote against the resolution.

Assignment

Deliver three speeches either supporting or opposing the resolutions of other group members. Since you must respond to points made in debate, these speeches will be primarily impromptu in nature. Still, as you will be able to view the agenda ahead of time, you can gather evidence on the issues being debated and prepare certain arguments ahead of time. Therefore, these speeches should also exhibit the characteristics of effective speech-making and reflect an understanding of the issues being discussed.

PRESIDING OFFICER:

Definition

The presiding officer runs the meeting. The main goal of this individual should be to guarantee fairness and equality for all members of the group. In order to serve as presiding officer, an individual must know parliamentary procedure, must be able to prevent violations in procedure, must recognize speakers in a fair and equitable manner, and must make sure debate alternates between speeches supporting and opposing a resolution.

Assignment

At the beginning of each meeting, a presiding officer will be elected. If you are elected to serve in this position, this responsibility will take the place of two supporting or opposing speeches. It will be the responsibility of the presiding officer to run the meeting and to meet all of the requirements stated above.

SAMPLE RESOLUTION

A Resolution Concerning Mandatory
Speech Classes in Public High Schools

Whereas: Speech is an important aspect of daily life, and

Whereas: The ability to speak well improves a person's chances to succeed in school and in a career, and

Whereas: Effective communication is needed in government, business, the media, and education, and

Whereas: Speech skills also improve other communication skills, such as writing, therefore

Be it Resolved: That all high school students in American public schools should be required to take at least one speech class in order to graduate.

BIBLIOGRAPHY

Anderson, Ellen M. and Fred L. Hamel. "Teaching Argument as a Criteria-Driven Process." *English Journal.* Nov. 1991:43-49.

Bettinghaus, Erwin P. and Michael J. Cody. *Persuasive Communication.* 4th ed. New York: Holt, Rinehart and Winston, Inc., 1987.

Bytwerk, Randall L. "Impromptu Speaking Exercises." *Communication Education.* Apr. 1985:148-49.

Carlile, Clark S. and Dana Hensley. *38 Basic Speech Experiences.* 9th ed. Topeka: Clark Publishing, 1993.

Dance, Frank E. X. and Carol C. Zak-Dance. *Public Speaking.* New York: Harper & Row, Publishers, 1986.

DeVito, Joseph A. *The Elements of Public Speaking.* 4th ed. New York: Harper Collins, Publishers, 1990.

Fletcher, Leon. *How to Design and Deliver a Speech.* New York: Harper & Row, Publishers, 1985.

Gregory, Hamilton. *Public Speaking for College and Career.* New York: Random House, 1987.

Gronbeck, Bruce E., Raymie E. McKerrow, Douglas Ehninger and Alan H. Monroe. *Principles and Types of Speech Communication.* 11th ed. Glenview, IL: Scott, Foresman and Company, 1986.

Hoff, Ron. *"I Can See You Naked:" A Fearless Guide to Making Great Presentations.* Kansas City: Andrews and McMeel, 1988.

Holland, Jack B. and Virgil D. Sessions. *Oral Interpretation Drill Book.* Boston: Holbrook Press, Inc., 1968.

Huffman, Melody. "The Maze As an Instructional Instrument for Public Speaking." *Communication Education.* Jan. 1985:63-68.

Lee, Charlotte I. and Timothy Gura. *Oral Interpretation.* 7th ed. Boston: Houghton Mifflin Company, 1987.

Littlejohn, Stephen W. *Theories of Human Communication.* 2nd ed. Belmont, CA: Wadsworth Publishing Company, 1983.

Maars, Carol. *The Complete Book of Speech Communication: A Workbook of Ideas and Activities for Students of Speech and Theatre.* Colorado Springs: Meriwether Publishing Ltd., 1992.

Meyer, Janice Jones. "The Oral Composition of Poetry in the Beginning Interpretation Course." *Communication Education.* July 1983:308-11.

Minnick, Wayne C. *Public Speaking.* Boston: Houghton Mifflin Company, 1979.

Monroe, A. H. and D. Ehninger. *Principles of Speech Communication.* 7th ed. Glenview, IL: Scott, Foresman Publishers, 1975.

Pelias, Mary Hinchcliff. "Communication Apprehension in Basic Public Speaking Texts; an Examination of Contemporary Textbooks." *Communication Education.* Jan. 1989:41-51.

Pizzi, William T. *Encyclopedia of Crime and Justice.* Sanford H. Kadish, Editor in Chief. New York: The Free Press, a division of Macmillan, Inc., 1983.

Stuart, Cristina. *How to Be an Effective Speaker.* Lincolnwood, IL: NTC Business Books, 1988.

Verderber, Rudolph F. *The Challenge of Effective Speaking.* 7th ed. Belmont, CA: Wadsworth Publishing Company, 1988.

Weiss, Donald H. *How to Make an Effective Speech or Presentation.* New York: American Management Association, 1987.

Wolf, Allan. *Something Is Going to Happen: Poetry Performance for the Classroom.* Asheville, NC: Iambic Publications, 1990.

Work, William. "On Communication Apprehension: Everything You've Wanted to Know But Have Been Afraid to Ask." *Communication Education.* July 1982:248-57.

Zimmerman, Gordon I. *Public Speaking Today.* St. Paul: West Publishing Company, 1979.

ABOUT THE AUTHOR

Brent Oberg is currently a speech and English teacher at Highlands Ranch High School in Highlands Ranch, Colorado. He has taught speech and coached competitive speech and debate at the junior high, high school, and college levels. His competitive speech and debate students have won numerous individual awards and he has qualified various students to compete in the national tournament.

He holds a bachelor's degree in speech and English education from the University of Wyoming and a master's degree in communication from Regis University in Denver. As a student, he also competed in speech and debate and was a collegiate national finalist.

He lives in Highlands Ranch with his wife, Beth.

ORDER FORM

MERIWETHER PUBLISHING LTD.
P.O. BOX 7710
COLORADO SPRINGS, CO 80933
TELEPHONE: (719) 594-4422

Please send me the following books:

_____**Speechcraft #TT-B149** by Brent C. Oberg *An introduction to public speaking*		**$12.95**
_____**The Complete Book of Speech Communication #TT-B142** by Carol Marrs *Ideas and activities for speech and theatre*		**$12.95**
_____**The Art of Storytelling #TT-B139** by Marsh Cassady *Creative ideas for preparation and performance*		**$12.95**
_____**Mel White's Readers Theatre Anthology #TT-B110** by Melvin R. White *28 all-occasion readings for performance and storytelling*		**$14.95**
_____**Theatre Alive! #TT-B178** by Norman A. Bert, Ph.D. *An introductory anthology of world drama*		**$24.95**
_____**The Scenebook for Actors #TT-B177** by Norman A. Bert, Ph.D. *Collection of great monologs and dialogs for auditions*		**$14.95**
_____**One-Act Plays for Acting Students #TT-B159** by Norman A. Bert, Ph.D. *An anthology of complete one-act plays*		**$14.95**

These and other fine Meriwether Publishing books are available at your local bookstore or direct from the publisher. Use the handy order form on this page.

NAME: _____

ORGANIZATION NAME: _____

ADDRESS: _____

CITY: _____ STATE: _____ ZIP: _____

PHONE: _____

☐ **Check Enclosed**
☐ **Visa or MasterCard #** _____

Signature: _____ *Expiration Date:* _____

(required for Visa/MasterCard orders)

COLORADO RESIDENTS: Please add 3% sales tax.
SHIPPING: Include $2.75 for the first book and 50¢ for each additional book ordered.

☐ *Please send me a copy of your complete catalog of books and plays.*